THE HISTORICAL ORIGIN

OF

CHRISTIANITY

Cover Design by
Walter Williams

Back Cover Photo By
Lynnice Johnson

Illustrations By
Randy (Buddy) Alexander
and
Jennie Scott Washington

Printing History
First Printing Maathian Press, February 1993
Second Printing Maathian Press, November 1994
Third Printing Maathian Press, August 1998
Fourth Printing Maathian Press, September 2001
Fifth Printing Maathian Press, January 2004
Sixth Printing Maathian Press, August 2006
Seventh Printing Maathian Press, March 2009
Eighth Printing Maathian Press, September 2011

Library of Congress
Catalog Card Number 042230904
ISBN: 978-1-881040-08-8
Printed in the United States of America

THE

HISTORICAL

ORIGIN

OF

CHRISTIANITY

By

Walter Williams

MAATHIAN PRESS
P.O. BOX 377655
CHICAGO, ILLINOIS 60637
U.S.A.

DEDICATION

I dedicate this book to my grandmother, Beulah; my grandfather, Thomas; my mother, Louise, and my aunt, Zelma, whose hearts and hands shaped my life and character; to my first wife Delores, with whom my first 20 years as a husband and father gave me substance and direction; to my late wife, Carol, who shared my vision of the Ancient Egyptian Museum and Institute; to my daughter, Vienea, and my son, Henry, who have surpassed my expectations as descendants of Ancient Egyptians in their consciousness; to my students at the Ancient Egyptian Institute, whose support and dedication enhance every endeavor we attempt as Ancient Egyptians; to my four grandchildren, Latonya, Henry III, Rasheed Walter, and René, who are developing their Ancient Egyptian consciousness; and to all the women and men in my life who have come forth as the Goddess Isis and the God Horus (Osiris) to assist me in developing this offering of The Historical Origin of Christianity; *and to my scholars, especially Larry Adams, who have disciplined themselves and allowed me to be their teacher. And to Sun Ra, the great musician who inspired my life by bringing the Ancient Egyptians into my consciousness at an early age. I thank you all!*

ACKNOWLEDGEMENTS

I wish to thank the following people for their help in the publication of this book: Jerry Parker, Gregg Thompson, Robert D. Sommerville, Larry Adams, Jennie S. Washington, Randy (Buddy) Alexander, Lynnice Johnson, Marshall Fluker, Arnetta May, and Debbie and Randy Alexander.

Walter Williams

NOTE: *The author is aware of the absence of footnotes. A bibliography has been added for reference purposes.*

CONTENTS

ILLUSTRATIONS

WORDS FROM THE AUTHOR

WHY I WROTE THIS BOOK

I clearly remember growing up in Chicago and attending the local schools. As a young boy, the images that I had before me of successful role models were few. The book I remember reading in grammar school was *Little Black Sambo*. It left an indelible mark on my memory. This was what I was supposed to identify with and grow up to become.

Well, I grew up to become a musician. I played in the band at DuSable High School, and after graduation, I "gigged" around Chicago with a musician named Sun Ra. Sun Ra was very clear about who he was and who we were as "Negroes," as we were known then. He often told us, "We are descendants of the Ancient Egyptians. We are descendants of the richest culture that has ever existed on this planet." I did not realize at that time what a profound effect these words would eventually have upon the future direction of my life.

Nearly 20 years later, while touring Italy with my late wife, Carol, and her sisters, I was struck by the comments of our tour guide. During his commentary extolling the grandeur of the Roman Empire, he, somewhat matter-of-factly, affirmed that the culture of Rome was virtually nonexistent until the Romans traveled to ancient Egypt and learned of the marvelous and sophisticated achievements of the Ancient Egyptian civilization. This had a very rousing impact on me and brought back to my consciousness Sun Ra's claims of our Ancient Egyptian heritage. This was to stir in me an overwhelming desire to know, I mean really know—with a great deal more specificity—the true meaning of Sun Ra's words. This incident was to set into motion what has become, in years since, my life's journey. This journey was also to alter my view of world religion.

This was the beginning of a 20-year search for the truth. My life has been dedicated to researching and finding out all that I could to resurrect the Ancient Egyptian consciousness in myself and eventually in my people. We have gone from Africans/slaves to Coloreds to Negroes to Blacks, and now, thanks to a proclamation by one of our leaders, we are confused as to whether to call ourselves African-Americans, Africans-in-America, Afro-American or Black Africans, ad infinitum.

In all my research, I have kept coming back to the same thing: How did Pharaohs become Negroes? What was the psychological button that was pushed, and what happened to a people who had controlled a perfect government for over 9,000 years, that they became slaves to Europeans?

I offer this book in love and peace to the modern day descendants of the Ancient Egyptians, who, today, out of ignorance, are calling themselves Nubians, Sudanese, Ethiopians, Negroes, Blacks or African-Americans. It is offered for their spiritual enlightenment and as a guide to who they were, are, and can become.

As I began my search for the answer, I stumbled across a book, *The Outline of History, Volume I*, by H.G. Wells. It was in a music studio owned by my good friend, Chicago musician, Jimmy Ellis. This book had a picture of Serapis, the icon/image that was projected as the god-image of the conquering Greek, Ptolemy I, Lagi, called "Soter" (meaning "Savior"). It was an exact likeness of the image of the "redeemer/savior/messia" known in Christianity as "Jesus the Christ." As I continued to unravel the pieces of a gigantic puzzle, all the information pointed to one thing: this icon/ image was the predecessor of the Jesus the Christ image.

As I take you through the detailed progression of events that led to the creation of the image, as they actually happened, I hope that your awakening will come as mine did. I realized that for the last 2,000 years, we have been given a perverted view of our contribution to this world. I realized that the image we have been given to worship as our redeemer/savior/messia was that of the conquering Europeans.

This will not be an easy book to read. It will be like tearing away your flesh to realize that your "Christ/Savior" was created from the image of Ptolemy I, Lagi, an uncivilized European who tried to get himself accepted into our Ancient Egyptian ancestors' priest society.

This chronological treatise that I present to you within these pages will give you, the reader, the necessary information to understand why the people of color on this planet have labored for the last 2,000 years believing that we were less than everyone else. It wasn't just the conquering

Europeans who damaged us. They had assistance from the Melchite Coptic Egyptians (the "Uncle Toms" of Antiquity) who cooperated with them to bring about this farcical deity, thereby causing themselves to be our worst villains.

The same damage to our African community is being repeated every Sunday morning from the pulpits of Christian churches all over America and the world. Consider how these Christian ministers hold before their congregations the icon/image of Jesus Christ and reiterate over and over that this is our Lord, God and Savior. They are encouraging us to worship this European image which causes us to become the principle agent in our own spiritual destruction and confusion. We end up hating ourselves as a race of people and each other individually, but loving and emulating the European race.

As we approach the 21st century and continue to search for answers to the fulfillment of a people—us—we must examine all that happened, from the time the Greeks invaded Egypt in 332 B.C.E., through the convoking of the subsequent councils that were called and attended by our Coptic Egyptian ancestors. These councils will give you the insight needed to understand the many fallacies that have been presented to us throughout the past 2,000 or more years.

As you examine this information, it will also lead you to understand that if we are to escape the bondage and the destruction of Christianity and all other man-made religions, such as Islam, Judaism, Buddhism, etc., we must resurrect ancient Egypt into our consciousness. We must share with our children the greatness of their ancestors and never again allow those misguided "brothers" and "sisters" in our midst to compromise our relationship with the Creator.

I urge you to read and study this book very carefully. It will not be easy reading because of its unfamiliar terms, times, people and places. I have included a glossary and bibliography to assist the learning process. This book also will not be easy reading because of its untraditional and challenging perspective. I am aware of the repetition in this book, but it is there to help you understand the message.

Walter Williams

PREFACE

It will, no doubt, be difficult for some individuals to imagine that the genius within this book was created by someone who does not fit the mold of most of the world's historians of ancient and classical history. The author does not come with a traditional "formal" education from the better educational institutions in the world. Perhaps this may be precisely the spirit, daring and free thought that is necessary to bring forth new scholarship in the area of Ancient Egyptian history. And this is exactly what Walter Williams, along with his associates who share his dream, have done. His dream is to resurrect the Ancient Egyptians and the many achievements of the Ancient Egyptian civilization into our consciousness. He wants to cause a resurgence of this knowledge into the hearts and minds of Ancient Egypt's present day descendants. These present day descendants are known in the world today as Nubians, Sudanese, Ethiopians, African-Americans, Blacks, and Negroes, especially here in America. We as a people need to be mindful of the names we allow to be attached to us because all such names have a history attached to them. The names Negro, black or African-American all have a non-ethnic "slave in America" identity.

It is said that a journey begins with the first step. This book creates a quantum leap in the area of Ancient Egyptian history as it pertains to the historical origin of Christianity. It provides new scholarship in understanding the true history of Christianity and the dominant role that our ancestors played in it.

Robert D. Sommerville
Historian-Researcher
Chicago, Illinois

INTRODUCTION

As we approach the dawn of a new century, the Western communities continue to consolidate themselves politically, economically and militarily. Yet the power behind these societies goes far beyond their military bases. The key to Western power can only be gauged by its ability to control people throughout the world. To that end, the Western world has incorporated a philosophy of psychology, where myths, lies and deception are the order of the day and death and destruction are the Western ways of life.

Historically, as you progress through time, you will eventually encounter a powerful triad of religions: Christianity, Islam and Judaism. All of these religions have had strong mass appeal and persuasive powers, and they remain the most powerful tools in the Western world's arsenal of controlling forces. These religions serve as the ultimate sentry for Western world interests. They were developed and are perpetuated to preserve past gains, enhance present gains, and ensure future gains.

Contrary to popular belief, Christianity serves as the foundation for both Islam and Judaism. To understand the historical origin of Christianity is to understand the true nature and purpose of religion. To understand religion is to take it out of the romantic, the mysterious, and the mystical and expose it as having no historical realism or boundaries. The only boundaries these religions have are that of the writers' imagination.

Whether you set these religions in a present or historical setting, where their true attributes can be extracted and displayed, you will find these attributes to be cold, calculated, deceptive and devious lies. Western religion is the ultimate deceptive psychological ploy, primarily because religion professes to encompass the word of GOD. Therefore, to accept another religion over a Western religion is to be ridiculed and reduced to an uncivilized savage. To deny these Western religions altogether is to damn your soul to eternal suffering.

Cosmetically, these religions are embodied with high principles and valued ideas, but underlying this surface is the most devastating psychological ploy imaginable. Unsuspectingly, believers offer little resistance to their acceptance of these religions because, typically, religion is introduced to them by their parents. The orchestration and embellishment of these religions are a primary function of the mass news media to visually bring myths and lies to life, to lend validation to them and make them believable in the eyes of the masses. To fuse religion with the mass media is to mathematically multiply and accelerate religious appeal. The mass media have caused a chain reaction so encompassing in its effectiveness that very few escape its trap. We are bombarded with tens of thousands of messages a year and are repeatedly subjected to such techniques as the power of suggestion, the power of association, reverse psychology and reward and punishment. These subliminal suggestions are categorically reinforced by every major institution of the Western world, from the educational system to the news media, from the religious institutions to the movie industry, and from the legislative, judicial and executive branches of government. This begins to explain why people throughout the world have accepted these religions so wholeheartedly.

To further expose the deceptive nature of these psychological ploys, let's examine an example of reverse psychology: With reverse psychology, you have an exchange of roles and a reversal of fortune.

On an historical level, this scenario is played out to the nth degree. The table was turned on the creators of civilization—THE ANCIENT EGYPTIANS— and their descendants who now call themselves African-Americans, Blacks, Negroes, Nubians, Sudanese, Ethiopians, etc. These are the people who created and developed animal husbandry, agriculture, cosmetics, internal medicine and mortuary science, the calendar and the world's first democracy. These are the people who created the natural sciences, including biology, chemistry, physics, astrology and astronomy. They also created mathematics encompassing arithmetic, algebra, calculus, geometry and trigonometry. They invented architecture and civil and mechanical engineering. Finally, and probably most significantly, these are the people who invented writing and the world's first three alphabets, which include the hieroglyphic, the hieratic script, and the phonetic script. Every alphabet used in the world today is based on one of these three alphabets created by the Ancient Egyptians.

These claims are manifest in the fruits of their labor which stand today as a testament to their greatness. They are documented by the following monuments and inventions:

- *The massive pyramid complex at Giza.*

- *The great temples at Karnak and Luxor.*

- *The royal tombs at the Valley of the Kings.*

- *The mortuary temple at Deir el-Bahri and Remesseum.*

- *The mortuary temple at Abu Simbel.*

- *The building of boats for long distance travel.*

- *Mummification.*

These monuments and inventions collectively embody all of the scientific and mathematical principles previously mentioned and are the foundation for all modern scientific research. They imply mathematical and scientific principles yet to be rediscovered for these awesome structures and inventions cannot be duplicated, even with today's technology. These great technological feats are just half of the equation that constitute the creators of civilization. The other half is their humanity and spirituality.

Since the inception of the Ancient Egyptian civilization, the people of Egypt incorporated what is known as the Maathian Creed in every aspect of their lives. This creed encompasses the concepts of peace, love, wisdom, truth and justice.

Unlike some European cultures that later obtained the level of technological advancement through assimilation, the Ancient Egyptians never oppressed the people they visited. To the contrary, they elevated the people they visited with respect to their culture. This is evidenced by the people of India, China, Central America and North America. All of these civilizations started at the point at which they came into contact with the Ancient Egyptians.

With the stroke of a pen, the descendants of these incredible people were diminished to Negroes, buffoons, subhumans, nonhuman animals and slaves. A permanent slave class or race was created. Slavery was given an inferiority label and an African identity to the extent that the two became synonymous. Africa equaled slavery and slavery equaled inferiority.

We must remember that there is nothing innate about slavery, but there is something innate about those who would enslave. Slavery is not a matter of intelligence, race or social status; it is a matter of policy and politics. Policy is defined as a plan or course of action, as in a government, political party or business, designed to influence and determine decisions. Politics is defined as the execution of policy. Therefore, slavery requires three things: the victim, the policy and the mechanism to enforce the policy.

Malcolm X said it best: "Just because Europeans are the dominant race does not mean they are superior, but means that they are the most brutal and will stop at nothing to maintain the status quo."

With the same pen that demoted the creators of civilization, the nomadic, barbaric people of Europe used this same pen to elevate themselves to royal status and stole credit for most of the collective knowledge of the world. Never mind the principles of government, science, mathematics and economics that had been established thousands of years before the first European came on the scene of history. Never mind that Europeans migrated into the land area known today as Egypt and absorbed the Ancient Egyptian culture and its high civilization already in place. With a brutal military force and an uncanny ability to deceive, lie and trick, the impostors of civilization were able to make that which was good bad and that which was bad became good.

The reverse psychology process is now complete. It is important to know that Christianity, and religion in general, is binate. It is also important to note that religion embodies a preset value system and it is the engagement of this value system that we see on two levels (political and esoteric).

Christianity and other religions are the instruments of political and social control. They are the mechanism by which western governments exercise direct and indirect control over their populations. This is the basic political level. On the other hand, the esoteric level holds a special problem for those persons who are of African origin. For it is these people who embrace religion wholeheartedly.

When you adopt a god who is not in your own image, when you embrace literature that teaches you to hate yourself and love your enemy, when your oppressor and savior and your god and enslaver are one and the same, you become the principal agent in your own destruction. Your spiritual and physical death are a foregone conclusion.   God on earth is the illusion of white supremacy because white supremacy is ultimately the embodiment of the European as god in the form of the incarnated Logos "Christ."

What you are about to witness is the unveiling of the greatest lie ever told.   The creation of Christianity and the incarnated Logos "Christ" was not an act or an event; it was a process, a process that took more than 700 years to evolve. It was a process that took the image of the Greek Ptolemy I, Lagi, and ultimately transformed it into the pseudo-messias   or   "(K)Christos-Christ." Unfortunately, some of our Coptic Egyptian ancestors played a critical part in this charade, but it is inspiring to know that the majority of this community resisted the encroachment of this man-made entity, to the point of death, generation after generation.

Walter Williams will take you through a step-by-step progression of historical events that ultimately resulted in the formation of Christianity. Walter's perspective is unique and new because it is completely void of biblical writing and influence. If there is one idea that Walter Williams has propounded, it is that Christianity, like all other religions, is man-made not spiritually inspired.

Within the pages of this book, you will learn when, where and how Christianity came about. You no longer have to suspend your common sense or analytical powers or be afraid to question the so-called "Word of God."

Walter Williams is the vanguard of investigative research and new scholarship. I invite your active participation by reading every powerful line. I challenge you to dismiss your fears and use your analytical ability to its greatest extent.   T h e cycle has been broken. Walter Williams has successfully circumvented the elaborate web of lies, tricks and perverted scholarship used to control the whole world.

In conclusion, *The Historical Origin of Christianity* is a profound achievement in investigative research. It is uniquely bold, penetrating and liberating. The author has transcended the myths that have entrapped the majority of the scholarly community since the advent of the so-called European Renaissance. Although these deceptions did not originate in Renaissance Europe, it was during that period that they were fused with political intent and taken to a new dimension.

A classical analysis of self-incriminating European philosophy is poignantly brought to life through the work of Niccolo Machiavelli, an Italian statesman and Renaissance writer. In his book entitled *The Prince*, Machiavelli explains that the European mind set is one of corruption, treachery and duplicity. Among Europeans, these practices are endorsed and highly recommended as a means for achieving any desirable end.

Whereby the end always justifies the means and the end is always related to the acquisition of political power and control, this formula (which was so much a part of European thinking during the Renaissance era) can be divulged as the same critical glue that holds together the illusionary facade of the Western world today.

CHAPTER I

IN THE BEGINNING
WAS THE PERSECUTION

In order to understand the historical origin of Christianity, one dominant fact must be understood. This fact is that, to this day, there is no historical data or biography in existence to substantiate the life and times of a Jesus the Christ. As John L. McKenzie, S.J., states in his book, *Dictionary of the Bible*, p. 432:

"The writing of the life of Jesus has been the major problem of NT scholarship for more than a hundred years; after numerous shifts of opinion, the consensus of scholars is that the life of Jesus cannot be written. The reason is that the data for a historical biography do not exist...the only sources of the life and teachings of Jesus are the four gospels. The contents of the Apocryphal gospels are historically worthless."

The meaning of the word *apocryphal* is *"ficti-tious books of uncertain authorship,"* such as the four apocryphal gospels of Matthew, Mark, Luke and John. But the main reason for not having historical data or a biography for a Jesus the Christ is because *there has never been a man that ever walked the earth in human form of any race, creed or color, by the name of Jesus Christ.* Let's go a little deeper and find out how, when and where did this created icon/image known as Jesus Christ come about.

It started with the invasion of Alexander the Greek into Egypt in 332 B.C.E. (see glossary), at which time he removed the existing Pharaoh gover-nor and put himself in his place. At the same time, he demanded that the Ancient Egyptian priest society relate to him as a god and give him priest status and accept him into their sacred institutions, which would have given him legitimacy. His demands were rejected because the Ancient Egyptians did not worship human form. They paid homage to their ancestors and nature. They were also in tune with universal spiritual consciousness, a direct spiritual link with the Creator. Alexander, and later the Ptolemies and the Romans, knew that in order to rule Egypt and its people, they had to be accepted and made part of the Ancient Egyptian sacred soci-

ety. However, the Ancient Egyptians considered
Alexander a spiritually out-of-tune, uncivilized
European alien and, therefore, his efforts were
rejected. Also there is no evidence to suggest that
the Ancient Egyptians accepted persons of other
races or cultures into their sacred priest society, and
thus, Alexander's demand that they receive him as
a god was the world's first form of European racial
supremacy (i.e., racism).

At the time of Alexander's death in 323
B.C.E., Ptolemy I, Lagi (also called "Soter") took
over the rule of Egypt. It is very important to note
that the word "Soter" means "Savior" (a title given
to Ptolemy I, Lagi, as a result of his military
conquest). The word "Savior" plays a significant
role in the evolution of the created image called
Jesus Christ and the man-made, non-spiritual
religion called Christianity.

Ptolemy I, Soter, like Alexander, also tried to
get himself accepted into the Ancient Egyptian
priest society. He was also rejected for the same
reason as Alexander. At this time in history (320
B.C.E.), Ptolemy I, Soter, sought out and found a
council of Ancient Egyptian priests and priestesses
in Memphis, Egypt who agreed to make his image
into a god. These Melchite Coptic Egyptians

complied with Ptolemy I's request and made a composite using two of their Ancient Egyptian gods, "Ausara" (Osiris), and the Sacred Bull of Memphis, "Apis," and during this process came up with the name "Oserapis," later Serapis. They then gave the name "Oserapis" to Ptolemy I, and gave his image the assimilated characteristics of their Ancient Egyptian Ancestor Ausara (Osiris) thereby making Ptolemy and his image a "god." They later created a devotional ritual to Serapis; he was spoken of as "The savior and leader of souls, leading souls to the light and receiving them again." The ritual goes on to say, "he raises the dead, he will save us after death and we will be protected in his providence." (See *Serapis, The Outline of History*, by H.G. Wells, Volume I.) Today, the same thing is being said about this created image called Jesus Christ who has a created birth date of 4 B.C.E. and a created death date of 28 or 30 A.B.C.E. (For an understanding of the use of the term A.B.C.E., see glossary.)

Allow me to emphasize that it was our ancestors, the Coptic Melchite Egyptians, who created the image of Serapis. This, in effect, was to be used later to create the religion of Christianity (by giving the Serapis icon/image a human nature through a dyophysitic union) which was officially done at the Council of Ephesus in 431 A.B.C.E. (See Chapter V, Council of Ephesus.)

After the Melchite Coptic Egyptian priests and priestesses in the temple of Memphis, Egypt fulfilled Ptolemy I's request and provided him an image of himself made into a god, man-made religion (not universal spiritual consciousness as practiced by the Ancient Egyptians) came into existence for the first time in human history. Ptolemy I, attempted to put this man-made icon/image of himself into all the sacred temples throughout Egypt alongside the Ancient Egyptian god, Osiris. This was his way of getting himself accepted into the Ancient Egyptian priesthood. However, as previously mentioned, this devious scheme of Ptolemy's was rejected by the entire sacred priest society throughout Egypt (except in Memphis, Egypt where the name Serapis and icon/image were created). Angered by this rejection, Ptolemy I, Soter, proceeded to close all other sacred Ancient Egyptian temples throughout Egypt and made it against the law for any Ancient Egyptian to build any temples or buildings for the purpose of spiritual fellowship. The closing

The Ancient Egyptian Ancestor, Ausara (Osiris)

down of our ancestors' sacred temples during the reign of Ptolemy I, Soter, completely eliminated the last of the pharonic sacred institutions of ancient Egypt. This was the beginning of the erosion of the spiritual unity that the Ancient Egyptian priesthood had tried to keep in place throughout Egypt during Egypt's occupation by the Greeks.

The passing of this law forced the priests and priestesses to use their homes for spiritual purposes. The law stayed in effect until the time of the Roman ruler Justinian I, who, in 543 A.C.E., along with his wife, Theodora, financed and built the world's first Coptic Christian Monophysite church in Syria today called the Jacobite Church. This church was built and later named for Jacob Baradaeus, a.k.a. James Baradai, the Coptic Egyptian quasi-Monophysite Christian who was appointed by Theodora to evangelize among the European Arabs. From monophysite christianity, the pagan religion of Mohammadanism/Islam was created. The Jacobite church followers only recognized the Osiris-like characteristics in the created image of the Serapis/Christ icon and thereby did not accept or recognize a human nature in this man-created icon.

The followers in the church were called Jacobite Monophysites (see Chapter V).

Subsequent to the closing of our ancestors' sacred temples throughout Egypt, Ptolemy I, Soter, confiscated all of their divine and sacred inspired writings which were written on papyrus scrolls, and proceeded to store them in the one remaining temple in Memphis, Egypt. This was the temple where his image had been made into the pagan god Serapis. Every Ptolemy ruler, and later Roman rulers, of Egypt sat on the throne of Egypt and became the Vicar of Serapis, just as the Roman Catholic pope of today sits on the throne of Peter in the Vatican and passes himself off as the Vicar of this created image called Jesus Christ.

It was Ptolemy I, Soter's grandson, Ptolemy III, Euergetes I, who built the Serapeum Temple and annex building in Alexandria, Egypt in 240 B.C.E. Today, this annex building is known in history as the Great Library of Egypt. This annex building became the Great Library of Egypt when Ptolemy III, Euergetes I, transferred the Ancient Egyptian divine scrolls into this annex building after removing them from the old temple in Memphis, Egypt where his grandfather, Ptolemy I, Soter, previously stored them. Thus, the annex became the Great Library of Egypt. This refutes the lie that is told about Alexander the Greek building the Great Library of Egypt to house the supposed thousands of books of the fictitious Aristotle, his supposed teacher. Aristotle is deemed fictitious because the Greeks during the time of antiquity did not have an alphabet nor institutions (see chapters VIII–IX). After removing the sacred scrolls from the old temple in Memphis, Egypt Ptolemy III, Euergetes I, began to tear down the old temple to make way for the new temple he was to erect in Memphis, Egypt to honor Serapis, called the Dionysian Temple. As we go further, you will see the significance of the annex building in the development of the man-made pagan religion called christianity (see Chapter IV).

As you follow Serapis throughout the Greek oc-cupation of Egypt, you will find another significant development in the creation of Christianity. At this time in history (197–196 B.C.E.), the Melchite Copts began to worship Serapis as a god, and at the same time giving honor to Ptolemy V, Epiphanes (Eucha-ritos), the Vicar of Serapis. The worship of Serapis and the honor given to Ptolemy V Epiphanes was created by a new generation of Melchite Coptic Egyptians who comprised the general council of Priests and Priestesses in the Dionysian Temple in

Memphis, Egypt. This honor to Ptolemy V was created to celebrate the first commemoration of the coronation of Ptolemy V, the King of Egypt and to give thanks for the many favors given by him to the Melchite Priest Society. The commemoration ceremony also established in history the religious ritual called the Eucharist. This ritual was also made part of Ptolemy V Epiphanes' title, which was Eucharistos.

This honor, the Eucharist, became the first order of service set aside in the religious temples that honored Serapis, such as the Dionysian Temple in Memphis, Egypt, the Serapeum in Alexandria, Egypt, and the Temple of Serapis in Canopus, as well as military installations throughout the land area ruled by the Ptolemies and later the Romans. *This Eucharist, bestowed upon Ptolemy V, Epiphanes, and Serapis, is still being used today by the Roman Catholic Church in its opening ritual service called the Mass/Communion Service.*

The Roman Catholic Church through its teachings of Christian theology has deceived the world population by teaching the believer to believe that the ritual called the Consecrated Eucharist which was a ritual created by the Dyophysitic Coptic

Egyptian Christians (see Chapter VII) is the "Lord's Last Supper," i.e., Serapis/Christ surrounded by twelve other European images at a banquet table supposedly eating the "last supper." This Eucharist as commemorated to Ptolemy V, Epiphanes (Eucharistos) and the image of Serapis has nothing to do with today's meaning of the Consecrated Eucharist. The question has to be asked, how was the ritual originally used? During and after the commemoration to Ptolemy V, Epiphanes, and Serapis, the Melchite Egyptian priesthood and the Greek occupants of Egypt, gave recognition to Serapis and Ptolemy V, Epiphanes by celebrating the Eucharist in their homes during the usual hour of dinner or late afternoon supper. To them, this was a time to be thankful and grateful to Serapis and Ptolemy V, Epiphanes, the Vicar of Serapis, for the many favors bestowed by Ptolemy V, Epiphanes, in the name of Serapis. To make way for this strong commemoration to Ptolemy V, Epiphanes, and Serapis, the Melchite Egyptian priesthood at Memphis removed all of the other remaining Ancient Egyptian deities from the three temples honoring Serapis. This left only the Serapis icon/image to be worshipped.

This elite, Melchite bourgeois class of Coptic Egyptians were like their brethren before them, the Council of Priests and Priestesses, who destroyed our beloved Ausara (Osiris) and Apis and created this European icon/image of Serapis during the reign of Ptolemy I, Soter using his image to do so. They were a group of traitors who betrayed our ancient ancestors for a few crumbs and favors from the uncivilized savage Greeks and later the heathen Romans thereby separating themselves from the masses.

The honor to Ptolemy V, Epiphanes (Eucharistos), is being used to this very day in the Roman Catholic Church and other religious institutions and is called the "Epiphany" or "Little Christ" or "Little Christmas." It is celebrated from December 26 through January 6, which is called the "Twelfth Night." This explains the historical origin of the "Epiphany." The same type of commemoration that was given to Ptolemy V, Epiphanes, had been given previously to Ptolemy III, Euergetes I, in 238 B.C.E. by the same Council of Melchite Coptic Egyptian priests and priestesses. However, apotheosizing the image of Serapis by using the ritual of the Eucharist was never accepted by the Exterior Coptic Religious

Community, only by the Melchite Copts who went along with the Greeks and later the Romans, for whatever reasons.

The next important step in the understanding of the pagan religion called Christianity is the historical time era of the five council meetings that transformed and made this created spiritless creature Serapis into the Messias ([K]Christos-Christ). The five council meetings I am referring to are the Council of Niceae I (325 A.B.C.E.), the Council of Constantinople I (381 A.B.C.E.), the Council of Ephesus (431 A.B.C.E.), the Council of Chalcedon (451 A.B.C.E.) and the Council of Constantinople II (553 A.C.E.). I will give an overview of these events by explaining what went on at each council meeting. Make note of the fact that these council meetings were convened by our Melchite Egyptian ancestors for the sole purpose of apotheosizing and making this created creature Serapis into the Messias and a god for the European World Community, and also to destroy the strong opposition from our Exterior Coptic Egyptian ancestors. During this time in history, any member of the Exterior Coptic Egyptian Religious Community was called an "Arianist" or a "Monophysite."

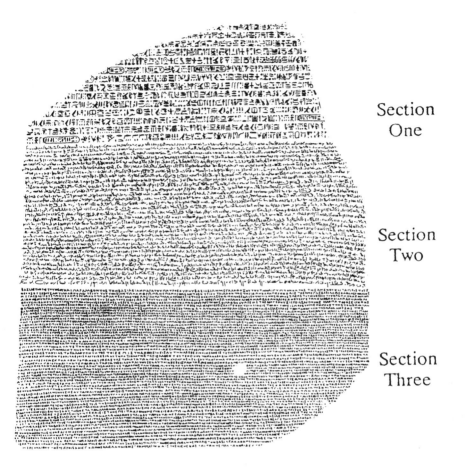

The Rosetta Stone

The Rosetta Stone showing the three (3) forms of writing of the Ancient Egyptians: section one - the Medu-Netcher or hieroglyphics, section two - the hieratic-demotic, and section three - the phonetic alphabet, today as a misnomer called the Greek alphabet.

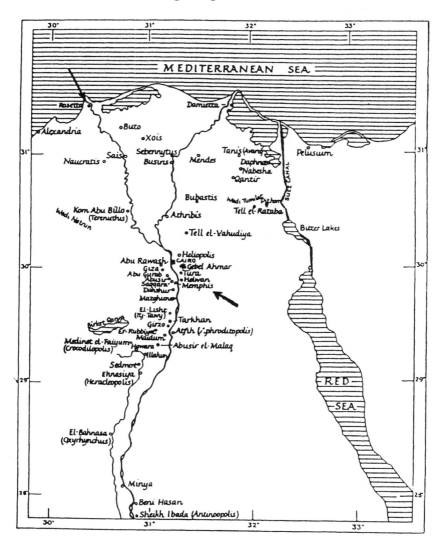

Map of Lower and Middle Egypt showing the city of Rosetta where the Rosetta Stone was found, and the city of Memphis where the image of Serapis was created.

Now let's investigate to develop an understanding of what our ancestors did at each of these council meetings to cause the creation of Christianity and the image of Serapis to become the Messias ([K]Christos-Christ). However, before doing so, it is important to discuss the three historical events that caused the first council, the Council of Niceae I (325 A.B.C.E.), to be called:

(a) The Donatist Schismatic Controversy;

(b) The Donation of Constantine;

(c) The Strong Statement by Arius.

Each event is discussed in the following chapter.

CHAPTER II

EVENTS LEADING TO THE COUNCIL OF NICEAE I

Donatist Schismatic Controversy

The first historical event that caused the Council of Niceae I (325 A.B.C.E.) to be convened was the "Donatist Schismatic Controversy."

"The Donatist Schismatic Controversy" was a dispute that affected and divided the Exterior Coptic Religious Community in North Central Africa and Northeast Africa during the fourth century. Donatism was primarily religious in origin. It began with a quarrel over the reconciliation of the traitors, clerics and bishops who were responsible in handing over their sacred writings to the Imperial Roman Emperor, Diocletian, during the Diocletian persecution (303-305 A.B.C.E.).

Questions were raised regarding the validity of the ordination conferred by bishops who had con-formed to the imperial demands. In particular, the actions of Bishop Mensurius of Carthage were challenged. He had satisfied the persecution authorities by handing over the sacred writings. His actions were considered sinful and immoral by the Exterior Coptic Religious Community who claimed that he should have offered himself to be martyred in the spirit of their predecessors during the Decian Persecution (250-251 A.B.C.E.). This thought received support from Bishop Donatus of Nigrae and Bishop Secundus of Tigisi, the Metropolitan of Numidia. They reasoned that the part played by the minister in the administration of the holy baptism for sanctity was substantial and not merely instrumental. Therefore, they maintained that a minister without grace could not confer the holy sacrament of baptism. Since they held that all persons outside the Coptic Religious Community lacked grace and holiness which was required in the ministry, sanctity could only be obtained inside of the Exterior Coptic Religious Community. For them, their religious community was an exclusive caste that should not be contaminated by contact with known sinners, least of all, with the infamous traitors who had handed over the sacred writings to be burned by the persecutors and who refused martyrdom. It was further declared that any bishop or clergy who communicated with the traitors should be cut off from the Exterior Coptic Religious Community and lose both his sacred character and the power to confer sanctity. The holy Coptic Exterior Religious Community contained no known sinners for it was absolutely separated from the world of sinners.

This schism caused the Exterior Coptic Religious Community to become weak and divided. This weakness and division gave Constantine I the devious idea and opportunity to once again offer this created European icon/image of Serapis to our ancestors, the Exterior Coptic Egyptians who had rejected this image at this time for 633 years. Constantine thought that this idea was a way not only to get Serapis accepted into the Exterior Coptic Religious Community, but himself as well, something that his predecessors before him could not do.

The Donation of Constantine

As a result of the Donatist Schismatic Contro-versy, the second historical event that caused the council of Niceae I (325 A.B.C.E.) to take place was offered. It is known today as "The Donation of Constantine." This was the idea of Emperor Constantine I who came up with the devious idea of wanting to expand the worship of Serapis throughout North Africa (Egypt, Libya, Tunisia, Algeria, Morocco and Mauritania), all of Europe, and all of Northeast Africa (today's Turkey, Syria, Jordan, Iran, Iraq, Saudi Arabia and Yemen). In order to do this, he needed the spiritual validation and support of the Exterior Coptic Religious Community. His idea was to get the Exterior Coptic Religious Community to apotheosize the image of Serapis just like their brethren the Melchites and to accept this image as a god and to use this religious community as an incubator for this purpose.

Constantine, at this point, had to find someone in the Exterior Coptic Religious Community to accept and go along with this idea. He approached Sylvester I who was a member of the Exterior Coptic Religious Community in Constantinople, Turkey. Turkey, at this time, had a large indigenous population of Coptic African Egyptians, as well as other parts of Northeast Africa. Note that for political reasons, today this area is known as the "Middle East." Sylvester I accepted the bribe from Constantine which contained the following:

(1) Constantine wanted to be, and was, baptized into the Melchite Coptic religious community in order to become a part of this community. *Note: This is what Alexander and the Ptolemies unsuccessfully tried to do for themselves.*

(2) After Constantine was baptized, he gave to Sylvester I his imperial power and authority over the people of this community (the Melchite and Exterior Coptic Religious Communities).

(3) By giving Sylvester I his imperial power, dignity and emblems, all on a temporal basis, this made the words and decisions of Sylvester infallible and inerrant. Having this imperial power, Sylvester was no longer a member of the Exterior Coptic Religious Community. The reason being is that the Exterior Coptic Religious Community rejected Constantine, Serapis and Sylvester I.

(4)   With this union, Sylvester became the new leader and head papa of the new Melchite Coptic Religious Community and Constantine became just a member. This donation also made Sylvester the world's first person of African origin other than a European to become the Vicar of the Serapis/Christ image. With this new title as the head of the Melchite Religious Community, his sole purpose was to get Serapis accepted by the Exterior Coptic Religious Community.

(5)   This union between Constantine and Sylvester brought about the Apostles' Creed, i.e., a reform creed. *Note: This reform creed is the original and true Apostles' Creed and should not be confused with the Apostles' Creed used today in Christian theology. This creed was originally established to reform the Exterior Coptic Egyptian Religious Community and remove*

Constantine I (274-337) Roman Emperor who gave the "Donation of Constantine" to Sylvester I.

Sylvester I wearing the Imperial Crown given to him by the Emperor Constantine after he accepted the "Donation of Constantine."

them from their established way of thinking and practice of paying homage to their Ancient Egyptian ancestors, Divine Triad of Osiris (the Father), Horus (the Sun) and Isis (the Holy Hathor Cow-Mother), a spiritual practice that was established by their Ancient Egyptian ancestors during the time of Antiquity. Instead, Sylvester wanted the Apostles' Creed put in its place to worship the European spiritless image of Serapis.

(6)   This Donation and union between Constantine and Sylvester I also made Sylvester what would be considered today in Christian theology, the pseudo-Apostle Peter. Constantine, as emperor and Vicar of Serapis gave his authority to Sylvester. *Note: Today, all popes of the Roman Catholic Church claim to get their papal authority from Peter and they claim Peter got his authority from Christ. As one can see, Constantine was the Vicar of Serapis and the image of Serapis*

later became the Messias ([K]Christos-Christ) at the Council of Ephesus (431 A.B.C.E.). Also recall how the created European image of Serapis was created by a council of Ancient Egyptian priests and priestesses in Memphis, Egypt (320 B.C.E.). They took two of our Ancient Egyptian gods, Ausara (Osiris) and Apis (Ra) and put them together as a composite to create the name Oserapis and gave the assimilated characteristics of Osiris to the image of Ptolemy I, Lagi, thus making the image of Ptolemy I a pseudo-god. All Greek and Roman rulers represented this false, spiritless image of Serapis as they ruled Egypt and parts of North and Northeast Africa beginning with Ptolemy I, Soter, and continuing with the Roman rulers. Just as the pharaohs of Ancient Egypt governed Egypt by representing themselves as Ausara (Osiris) thus keeping the Maathian Creed in balance with the priesthood in Egypt, similarly, the Greek and Roman rulers, represented themselves as the Vicars of Serapis.

At this point, Sylvester began to set up his own council of bishops and clergymen who went along with the bribe or donation. Together they started the foundation for the pagan religion called Christianity. This can be attested to by studying the council meetings of Niceae I 325 A.B.C.E., Constantinople I 381 A.B.C.E., Ephesus 431 A.B.C.E. and Chalcedon 451 A.B.C.E. From this study, one will be able to see how the created image of Serapis was made to be Christ and how the creation of the pagan religion called Christianity came into being. It took 751 years from the creation of the Serapis image (320 B.C.E.) to the Council of Ephesus (431 A.B.C.E.) to transform this European image of Serapis into the pseudo Messias ([K]Christos (Christ).

Therefore, the Council of Ephesus has to be used as the starting point for pseudo-Christ, and the Council of Chalcedon must be used as the beginning of the pagan religion called Christianity. If you are told about a Jesus Christ, Christians or Christianity before the Council of Ephesus (431 A.B.C.E.) or the Council of Chalcedon (451 A.B.C.E.), or even a Christian church before the building of the world's first Christian church, the Hagia Sophia (532 A.C.E.), you are being misled, on purpose or out of ignorance.

If the purpose of the Donation of Constantine had been accomplished during the life and reign of Constantine, he would have taken back the imperial and temporal power he bestowed upon Sylvester I and place himself as Caesar-O Papa over the Melchite and Exterior Religious Communities. His plan was to further spread this pagan worship of Serapis throughout Oriental North Africa, Northeast Africa and all of Europe with himself as the leader (Caesar-O Papa). This was to be done after the incubation and acceptance of Serapis by the Exterior Coptic Religious Community. However, this devious idea of Constantine's did not work during his life and reign mainly because of strong resistance from the majority members of the Exterior Coptic Religious Community. This dona-tion/bribe stayed in place in the Melchite Coptic Religious Community among some of its bishops and clergy until the reign of the Roman Emperor Justinian I. I will explain the role played by Justinian and his wife, Theodora, in Chapter VII - "The Council of Constantinople II."

Writers of history have hidden the real meaning and the true significance of the Donation of Constantine. They do this by using the names of Lorenzo Valla, Nicholas of Cusa and Caesar

Baronius for disqualifying purposes. In its place, the European religious scholar community has created the "Edict of Milan." This was done to make the world population think that there were Christians during the time of Constantine. One of the created stories that surrounds this fallacy is the story of how Constantine was supposed to have been converted to Christianity. The story states that in "312," on the eve of the battle on the Milvian Bridge near Rome, Constantine had the vision to which he attributed his conversion to Christianity. The story goes on to say that Constantine beheld a fiery cross in the heavens beneath which was written in Greek, "By this sign thou shalt conquer." However, Constantine also is said to have had a dream telling him to place the Greek monogram representing Christ (a combination of the letters X and P) upon the shields of his soldiers. The so-called legend continues to state that on the following day, Constantine was victorious, killing both Maxentius and his son, and as a symbol of victory, he adopted the monogram for his labrum (imperial standard). The story further states that in 313 A.D., Constantine published the Edict of Milan granting freedom of religion and stopping the persecution of the Christians. The story goes on to say that Constantine's reign marks a turning point in European history because he is, in a large measure, responsible for the fact that Christianity became the dominant religion in the Western world. Permit me to now explain why the Edict of Milan is a fallacy.

(1) As previously indicated, During the time and reign of Constantine I (306-337 A.B.C.E.), there was no Jesus Christ, therefore, no Christians or a religion called Christianity or a Christian church existing anywhere on the planet earth. The reason being is that the Serapis icon/image had not been made the Messias ([K]Christos) by the new Melchite Coptic Religious Community (see the Council of Ephesus).

(2) What actually happened is that Constantine made a promise to Sylvester I to stop the persecution of the Exterior Coptic Egyptian Religious Community if this community would accept the created

European image of Serapis as a god. This religious community had been under constant religious oppression and persecution beginning with Ptolemy I, Soter, which continued into the Roman era for their refusal to worship the European Serapis image.

A deal was made between Constantine and the metropolitan Coptic Egyptian Bishop of Constantinople, Sylvester I, who, at this time, was the exterior metropolitan bishop of the Coptic Exterior Religious Community in Constantinople, Turkey. Constantinople during this time had a large indigenous population of Coptic Egyptians. The deal was made between Constantine and Sylvester I to return the homes taken from members of the Exterior Coptic Religious Community and to stop persecuting this community if Sylvester I would accept what is known today in history as "The Donation of Constantine." The return of their homes was particularly significant because the Exterior Coptic Religious Community held their religious fellowship in two places: their homes and the cemetery. They were not allowed to build any buildings for religious purposes. Their homes were used for spiritual fellowship and the cemetery was used to honor their special dead, some of whom allowed themselves to be martyred by the Greeks and the Romans. In their honor, they built special structures called "Martyria," which were the world's first form of sepulcher tombs.

The Strong Statement by Arius

The devious idea of Constantine I to get Serapis accepted did not work during his reign and lifetime mainly because of the resistance from the majority members of the Exterior Coptic Religious Community. One such person was Arius, the Alexandrian presbyter, who, in 319 A.B.C.E., stated that the image of Serapis was a "created creature."

This was the third important historical event to cause the Council of Niceae I to be convened. The Strong Statement by Arius, stated that the image of Serapis was "a created creature, alien and dissimilar in all things from the Father (Osiris), a perfect creature above all other man-made creatures, but a creature nevertheless." This resistance started the Arianist and Monophysite movement against the Serapis image and continued with the coming of the European Arab Monophysite in the seventh century. The Arabs continued the resistance after being taught and introduced to Monophysite Christianity by the Coptic Egyptian (Jacob Baradaeus a.k.a. James Baradai). Eventually, this led to the iconoclasm controversy which caused the Council of Niceae II to be convened in 787 A.C.E. and continued into the Photius-Filioque schism 869–70 A.C.E. and the tenth century Bogomil schism. This resistance lasted until the name Mohammed first came on the scene of history and was given the same attributes of the Christ icon in 1240 A.C.E. Thus the man-made religion Mohammedanism was created, later to be called Islam. Today's history books are calling Arius a heretic. They are saying his strong statement about this creature Serapis, known today as Jesus Christ, was heresy. Nevertheless, Arius was right and today's historians are wrong.

The Alexandrian Presbyter Arius

The Donatist Schismatic Controversy, along with the Donation of Constantine and the strong statement by Arius caused the Council of Niceae I in 325 A.B.C.E. to be convened in Bithynia (modern Iznik, Northwestern Turkey in Northeast Africa). This meeting was held in the palace of Constantine. The Melchite Coptic Egyptians were now an organized council of hand-picked bishops and clergy. They were organized under the new head, Melchite Bishop Sylvester I, who called for this council meeting to be convened.

Now, let us proceed into each council meeting. But remember, each one of these council meetings was convened by the Melchite Coptic Egyptian papas, bishops, and clergy, except for the Council of Constantinople II in 553 A.C.E. which was called for by the Roman Byzantine Emperor, Justinian I. These council meetings were convened because of the opposing resistance of the Exterior Coptic Religious Community who rejected the image of Serapis as a god and repudiated Sylvester I for accepting "The Donation of Constantine." Keep in mind, these council meetings were convoked to make the created creature, Serapis, into the Messias ([K]Christos-Christ = Jesus the Christ).

CHAPTER III

THE COUNCIL OF NICEAE I

Let's begin with the first general council meeting, the Council of Niceae I (325 A.B.C.E.), also called the Nicene Council. The purpose of this council was to take the image of Serapis and insert it into the Ancient Egyptian Divine Triad to make it the son of Osiris, the father in the Ancient Egyptian Triad, thereby giving it a divine spirit.

This council opened at Niceae in Bithynia (modern Iznik, Northwest Turkey in Northeast Africa) in Constantine's palace with an opening address by the Emperor Constantine. About 300 bishops and clergy were present. Almost all were from the eastern half of Constantine's empire; more than 150 of them came from Northeast Africa, about 50 or more from Syria and 60 or more from Egypt and Libya, plus many other Coptic Melchite and Exterior Coptic clergy. Prominent figures were Bishop Hosius who presided with the delegates of Papa Sylvester I and Bishop Alexander who had publicly rebuked Arius. They brought charges against him for his strong statement and teaching against the creature Serapis. This dissension between Bishop Alexander and Arius began in the year 319 A.B.C.E. At this council, Constantine was given the honor of honorary president which allowed him to ensure peaceful discussions.

The first order of business was to circulate a petition among the bishops to condemn and excommunicate Arius and his followers. There was opposition among the bishops to signing such a decree. This opposition was crushed by the delegate bishops of Sylvester I who issued an ultimatum to either sign the decree or be given the penalty of banishment. Only two bishops from Libya refused, along with some Alexandrian clergy and virgins. As a result, Arius, who was not in attendance, and the two attending bishops who remained faithful to him, were anathematized, exiled, and banished. At this point, any member of the Exterior Coptic Religious Community who favored the position of Arius and his followers were called and considered *Arianists*.

The second order of business at this council meeting by the Melchite bishops was to insert the image of Serapis into the Ancient Egyptian Divine

Triad. This triad consisted of Ausara (Osiris) the Father, Horus the Sun and Auset (Isis, the Holy Cow Hathor) the Mother. This Divine Triad was used by the Exterior Coptic Religious Community in all of their religious practices which was the last remnant of the ancestor gods used by their ancestors, the Ancient Egyptians. Note: The old Melchite Copts gave Serapis the assimilated characteristics of Ausara (Osiris) in 320 B.C.E. and now at this council meeting, a new group of Melchite Copts under Sylvester I inserted this image of Serapis into the Ancient Egyptian Divine Triad and made this image the Son of the Father (the Father being Osiris). Serapis thereby took the place of Horus the Sun of Osiris and Isis in the Ancient Egyptian Divine Triad. This act was designed to give the creature Serapis a divine Osiris-like spirit.

Today, Christian theology teaches that Jesus Christ is the *Son* of Man, thus, you can see how this term came about, i.e., the term *Son* is man created and can always be applied to spiritless creatures created by man, such as Serapis/Christ. The term *Sun* is a Creator-given spiritual name given to Ausara (Osiris) and his *Sun* Horus by the

The Ancient Egyptian Divine Triad: from left to right, Horus (the Sun), Horus (Osiris), and Auset (Isis) the Holy Hathor Mother.

Ancient Egyptians who were spiritually in tune with the universe, which means *Sun* of the *Sun*, Ra, the Creator. This act of inserting Serapis into the Ancient Egyptian Divine Triad brought about the Homoousios Creed known today as the Nicene Creed. This Creed, devised by the Melchite Copts, added that Serapis was "from the substance of the father (Osiris)." "True God from True God, begotten, not made," i.e., "God the Father, God the Son, the Same." However, the key word of the Creed, which was to become so controversial for decades, was the term Homoousion Toi Patri, that is, "of One Substance with the Father." Thus, with the creation of the Nicene Homoousios Creed, Serapis became the Logos (the Word), the Incarnated Logos.

So, with the exile and banishment of Arius and his followers and the Nicene Creed established, this brought the Council of Niceae I to a close. Fifty-six years later, the second Ecumenical Council, called the Council of Constantinople I (381 A.B.C.E.), was convoked. It was held in Constantinople, Turkey (today called Istanbul) shortly after the baptism of the Roman Byzantine Emperor Theodosius I in 380 A.B.C.E. *Note: All Roman rulers had to be baptized in order to be made a member of the Melchite Coptic Egyptian Religious Community, beginning with Constantine I and continuing to the time of Justinian I. This was due to the provisions in the "Donation of Constantine" given by Constantine to Sylvester I.*

Let us now go to the second council called the Council of Constantinople I.

CHAPTER IV

THE COUNCIL OF CONSTANTINOPLE I

The Council of Constantinople I opened in a building in Constantinople, Turkey provided by the Roman Byzantine emperors Theodosius I and Gratian. *Note: The Melchite Religious Community had no buildings of their own for religious purposes. They used facilities provided for them by the Greek or Roman government.*

The Melchite Papa, Damasus, sent his legates to this council in which some 150 Melchite bishops of North Africa, Northeast Africa and Egypt met. The purpose of the meeting was to deal with the continued Arianist resistance against Serapis. The Exterior Coptic Religious Community was now considered Arianist because they practiced the views of Arius in not accepting the created creature Serapis as God. Therefore, the first order of business was to:

(1) Reaffirm the Nicene Homoousios Creed.

(2) Issue a decree to repudiate Arianism and Arianist thoughts among the Exterior Coptic Religions Community.

(3) Make the Nicene Homoousios Creed the official creed of the Byzantine Roman government.

(4) Recite this creed at the opening of all future council meetings thereafter, "God the Father, God the Son, the same."

(5) Favor Constantinople as the First See, in honor and dignity.

The council closed on July 9, 381 A.B.C.E. and, at the bishop's request, the Emperor promulgated its decrees on July 30.

Shortly after the close of this council meeting, Theodosius was totally unsympathetic to Arianism. He ordered the entire Exterior Coptic Religious

Community to profess the faith of the Melchite bishops of Constantinople and Alexandria, i.e., the Nicene Creed. He forbade the members of the Exterior Coptic Religious Community to meet for religious purposes and ordered the homes of their clergy seized.

His actions were criticized and stopped by the Melchite Coptic Bishop Ambrose of Alexandria. He reminded Theodosius that he had no power or authority over the Exterior Coptic Religious Community or the Melchite Religious Community due to the stipulations in the Donation of Constantine given to Sylvester I in 313-314 A.B.C.E. Theodosius accepted public humiliation at the hands of Bishop Ambrose and revoked the order to seize the homes of the Exterior Coptic clergy. He also revoked the order preventing them freedom to assemble.

During the rule of Theodosius I, a very important and tragic event happened. This happening was one of the main events in history that paved the way for the coming of the pagan, occult religion called Christianity. I am referring to the year 391 A.B.C.E. The place, Alexandria, Egypt, where a Melchite Coptic Egyptian theologian by the name of Theophilus, with the permission and encouragement of Theodosius I, destroyed the Serapeum Temple in Alexandria, Egypt; the Canopous Temple in the city of Canopus, Egypt; and the Temple of Dionysius in Memphis, Egypt. These were among the main temples honoring Serapis.

This destruction was done to make way for the Byzantine Roman government to keep the Nicene Homoousios Creed, but with a new name for Serapis. If you ask Christians throughout the world today if they have ever heard of Serapis, they will look at you with puzzlement and say "No." This is because Theophilus, the Melchite Coptic Egyptian and the Melchite Religious Community wanted to destroy the *name* "Serapis," but keep the *image* of Serapis, who was later at the Council of Ephesus (431 A.B.C.E.) renamed the Messias/(K)Christos/Christ.

The most tragic part of the actions of Theophilus was the destruction of the Serapeum Temple and annex building in Alexandria, Egypt. This annex building is known today as the Great Library of Egypt. The storage of our Ancient Egyptian ancestors sacred writings made this annex building to be called the Great Library of Egypt. With the destruction of this annex building by

The Melchite Coptic Egyptian Theophilus

Theophilus, thousands upon thousands of our Ancient Egyptian ancestors' divinely inspired scrolls and manuscripts were destroyed. As previously mentioned, these manuscripts and scrolls were taken from the sacred temples throughout Egypt after the temples were ordered closed by Ptolemy I, Soter—who ordered them closed because our ancestors refused to worship the image that was created and named "Serapis" after his image. Because of this action by Theophilus, over 500,000 inspired scrolls and manuscripts went up in smoke. These sacred works were the first literature written by man to ever exist on earth that could be deemed and called writings inspired by the Creator. Why? Because the Divine Creator used our ancestors, the Ancient Egyptians, as human instruments to create through and bring forth civilization for the entire planet and to be the keepers and messengers of cosmic Maathian universal laws of truth, justice, peace, love and wisdom. Note, the Ancient Egyptians being the first and oldest civilized people on earth invented the alphabet and a writing system along with the pen, ink and papyrus paper thereby being the only people on earth during the time of antiquity who were literate.

We now move to the most important of all of the ecumenical council meetings: the council called the Council of Ephesus.

CHAPTER V

THE COUNCIL OF EPHESUS

The most important of all the ecumenical councils was the Council of Ephesus which occurred (431 A.B.C.E.) 50 years after the Council of Constantinople I. At this council, the European icon/image of Serapis was transformed into the Messias ([K]Christos) by the Melchite Coptic Egyptians. Let us take a look at this council:

It was the third ecumenical council, held at Ephesus in Northeast Africa (Turkey) in 431 A.B.C.E. This council was called because of the difficulties provoked by the preaching of Nestorius, the quasi-Melchite, quasi-Monophysite, and his followers against the Title of Theotokos (the Mother of God) which was applied to the created creature—The Virgin Mary and by the Monophysitic teachings of Eutyches.

Nestorius preached that the Serapis image had one divine Osiris-assimilated spirit therefore the son of man but no human nature and thus could not be called a god. This preaching along with Monophy site teachings prompted the Council of Ephesus to come into being. The Melchite Bishop Cyril of Alexandria, who was commissioned by the Melchite Coptic Papa Celestine I, journeyed to Ephesus to preside at the council convoked by the Emperor Theodosius II at the request of Celestine. Celestine sent other legates with Bishop Cyril to preside over the council in his place with strict orders to conduct themselves in accordance with Cyril's instructed guidelines. The first objectives of the Melchite Copts were to reaffirm the Nicene Homoousios Creed, condemn Nestorius and Eutyches and their followers, and to devise and establish as official doctrine a human nature for the Serapis icon.

This was done by Cyril following the guidelines set forth by Celestine. Cyril maintained that the being (Physis - of the Word) had not undergone any change in becoming flesh. The Word (Logos) is united according to the substance (Hypostasis) to flesh animated by a rational soul. He is called the "Son of Man" where the two natures are joined in a true union and the two constitute one person and the one Son. The difference in natures is not suppressed by the Union, but the inexplicable meeting of divinity and humanity produces one sole Serapis/Christ. The Word was born of the Virgin and took to himself the nature of his own proper flesh.

This decree was supposed to have given Serapis a human nature which, in truth, was done by removing our Ancient Egyptian Goddess Auset (Isis) from the Ancient Egyptian Divine Triad and replacing her with a man-made created creature today called the Virgin Mary. This creature called the Virgin Mary was given the assimilated characteristics of Isis, thereby making this creature a goddess[1].

The European male, created-creature called Serapis had to be said to have been born through the body of a woman in order for this creature to have a human nature and body. So at the Council of Ephesus, the Melchite Coptic legates, following the orders of Celestine (carried out by Cyril), made a hypostatic union of this creature called the Virgin Mary with that of Serapis. Thus, this created creature called the Virgin Mary became the Virgin Theotokos—"The Mother of God"—thereby claiming the Logos (Serapis) had become flesh.

---

[1]Note: The Melchite and the Exterior Coptic Religious Communities practice celibacy during this time, calling their female members virgins.

Fig A.   Goddess Isis and Horus (The Sun)

Fig. B.   The two man-made created creatures, the Virgin Mary and Serapis (Christ, the Son of Man).

Fig. A.   A bust of Serapis wearing a crown of bough thorns and a grain modius on the head.   The grain modius gave the image the assimilated characteristics of the Ancient Egyptian God, Osiris.

Fig. B.   A head of Serapis, crowned with the bough thorns and modius grain cup.

Fig C.   The crucified Christ, wearing the bough thorn crown.

With this man-made dyophysitic (divine and human) nature of the created Logos (Serapis) and the created creature, the Virgin Mary as Theotokos, there began the development of a new theology. The Melchite Copts who spoke a Coptic Greek language made the Serapis image the "anointed Messias" and the word Messias in Coptic Greek means "(K)Christos"—and in English, "Christ." This caused the Melchite Community to become the world's first Dyophysitic Christians who in today's history books are being called "Coptic Christians."

Today, this contrived, spiritless creature called Serapis is worshipped throughout the world and is called Jesus the Christ, or Jesus, Son of Mary, the Savior and Redeemer of Mankind.

Now you can see how the image of Ptolemy I, Lagi called Soter (Savior) after receiving the composite names of Osiris and Apis was created and named (O)Serapis in 320 B.C.E. in Memphis, Egypt—who then was transformed into a god after receiving the assimilated characteristics of Osiris. You can also see how, during the Council of Ephesus, this creature Serapis was transformed into the Christ 751 years later. You can now see how the name Soter, which means savior, coming from Ptolemy I, Lagi played such an important part in the man-made religion called Christianity. Finally, you can see how this man-created icon called Serapis came to be called the Christ who today is called the Savior.

The fourth and next ecumenical council meeting was convoked 20 years later and was called the Council of Chalcedon.

CHAPTER VI

THE COUNCIL OF CHALCEDON

The fourth ecumenical council, held at Chalcedon from October 8 to 31, 451 A.B.C.E., marks a final episode in the quarrels over doctrine and policy that followed the Council of Ephesus (431 A.B.C.E.).

It now seemed necessary to complete the work of the Council of Ephesus by settling the question once and for all as to the one or two natures in Serapis/Christ. The bishops summoned to the council first met at Niceae, but were soon transferred to Chalcedon. However, the first order of business was to reaffirm the Nicene Homoousios Creed and to denounce the Nestorians, Monophysites, and Arianist who refused to recognize and call the created creature the Virgin Mary "Theotokos." Their intentions were also to denounce Eutyches, the Monophysite Arianist, who recognized only one nature in Serapis/Christ after the Hypostatic Union was made at the Council of Ephesus.

The Council of Chalcedon was presided over by legates who were sent by the Melchite Coptic Papa, Leo I. They had developed a new formula of faith by explicitly defining the two natures of Serapis/Christ which conformed to Papa Leo I's way of thinking.

This formula of faith was brought forth by the legates of Leo I in opposition to those who would destroy the Mystery of the Incarnation by partitioning Serapis/Christ. It also opposed those who refused to call the creature Mary "Theotokos" (the Nestorians).

And it opposed those who claimed that divine nature is incapable of suffering. And lastly, it opposed those who refused to recognize the amalgamation of the two natures and who spoke of only one nature after the Dyophisitic Union (Eutyches).

This council defined one Christ, Perfect God and Man, consubstantial with man, one soul being into two natures without division or separation and without confusion or change. However, the union does not suppress the difference in natures. Their individual properties remain untouched and they are joined together in one person, or hypostasis.

Jesus

Serapis and Jesus are one in the same, man-made created spiritless creature. (See Outline of History *by H.G. Wells, Volume I.)*

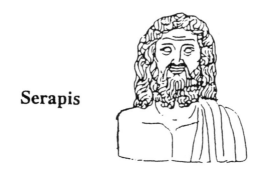

Serapis

This created creature was created in Memphis, Egypt in 320 B.C.E. after the image of Ptolemy I, Lagi called Soter (Savior).

This definition of the formula of faith, distinguished between nature and person, and stated that in Serapi/Christ there were two distinct natures whose individual properties had not been destroyed in the union. They subsisted in the unity of one person, or hypostasis.

This precision of vocabulary gave the word prosopon (person) a much stronger significance. It completed the Theology of Cyril with that of Leo I and definitively proclaimed the unique person of Serapis/Christ as the "*Son* of God" (Osiris) and the Son of the created-creature Mary, i.e., True God and True Man.

At this point, the council ended by consummating the concluded decree that was issued at the Council of Ephesus saying that the created-creature, the Serapis image, was the anointed Messias ([K]Christos) and the created creature, the Virgin Mary was the Theotokos (the Mother of God).

At this time in world history (451 A.B.C.E.), the man-made pagan religion, today called Christianity officially began, and the man-made icon creatures, today called Jesus, the Son of Mary, called the Christ, and the Virgin Mary had been consummated without further argument, i.e., the man-made pagan religion called Christianity began along with Serapis/Christ being brought forth as the object of worship of this new religion. *Note: This sets the first stage for the image of Serapis/Christ and the new developing Christian religion which was to be used as a political tool by, first, the Roman Byzantine ruler Justinian I and, later, the Roman Byzantine Catholic Church, the Hagia Sophia.*

The fifth council meeting to take place was called the Council of Constantinople II (553 A.C.E.).

CHAPTER VII

THE COUNCIL OF CONSTANTINOPLE II

The Council of Constantinople II came into being 102 years after the Council of Chalcedon in 553 A.C.E. This is the council that Emperor Justinian I convoked in the Great Hall of the Hagia Sophia in Constantinople. Its supposed purpose was to render final condemnation, in accordance with Justinian's earlier instructions on the Three Chapters or the three Nestorian Monophysite Chapters written by the African Bishops Theodore of Mopsuestia, Theodoret of Cyr, and Ibas of Edessa. The term "The Three Chapters" refers to the Edict of Justinian (544 A.C.E.), anathematizing certain chapters written against the Monophysites and Nestorians which were accepted and made part of the dogmatic laws at the Council of Ephesus.

In 542 A.C.E. Theodore Ascidas, a Dyophysitic Melchite Coptic Egyptian Christian and an advisor to Justinian, counseled Justinian that by condemning the three deceased bishops, he would gain favor and cooperation with the Monophysites. And at the same time cause distress and resistance from the person (Papa Vigilius) who had ecclesiastical authority in the Melchite community and the Hagia Sophia due to the Donation of Constantine. With resistance coming from Vigilius, Justinian was told he could use this as an excuse to take back the Donation of Constantine and give himself full ecclesiastical power. This was prompted by Justinian's desire to be the Ecclesiastical head of the world's first Christian and Roman Byzantine catholic (Universal) Church and Institution called the "Hagia Sophia" or the Church of the Blessed Wisdom. Today, the Blessed Wisdom is another name for Jesus the Christ.

Construction of this Church began in 532 and was finished 537 in Constantinople, today called Istanbul, Turkey, in honor of the created spiritless icon/image of Christ, today called Jesus the Christ. Justinian built this church, the Hagia Sophia, because he and his wife, Empress Theodora, planned to fulfill the dream of Constantine. The dream which Constantine did not live to see fulfilled was to take back the Donation of Constantine that was given to the Melchite

Coptic Egyptian Bishop Sylvester I on a temporal basis in 313-314 A.B.C.E. This was to occur if and when Sylvester could get the Serapis icon accepted by the Exterior Coptic Religious Community. However, Constantine's dream was partially fulfilled 118 years later by the Melchite Copts who apotheosized Serapis as the Messias and God at the Councils of Ephesus and Chalcedon.

But before taking back the Donation of Constantine, Justinian allowed the Melchite Dyophysitic Coptic Christian Religious Community to use this church for religious and teaching purposes. The idea was to set into place a religious ritualistic format in honor of Christ to be used when he took full ecclesiastical control of the Hagia Sophia. This was first done by creating oral Floriligia narrative homilies concerning Christ and was aided by them creating other rituals such as the ritual of offering bread and wine as the body and blood of Christ and calling it the "Consecrated Eucharist," the continued practice of celibacy for the priest society which identified their female members as virgins and also the use of the Nicene Homoousios Creed at all mass communions. All of the aforementioned rituals that were first created by the Coptic African Melchite Christians are used today in the Roman

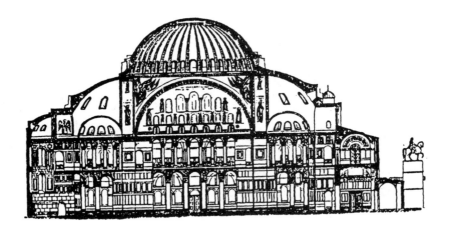

The Hagia Sophia

A section of the Hagia Sophia, The world's first Christian and Roman Catholic (Universal) Church, built in 532 A.C.E. in Constantinople, Turkey by Justianian I, also called the Church of the Blessed Wisdom.

Catholic Church. After this was done, Justinian decided that the Melchite Copts were no longer needed. He began to usurp their power of religious authority. This usurped power has continued and is used today by the Roman Catholic church in the Vatican.

At the close of the Council of Constantinople II, Justinian began to practice Caesaropapism and took on the role of pope with full ecclesiastical authority. Thus, in essence, he became the world's first European pope of the world's first Christian church (the Hagia Sophia) and the protector of the Melchite Coptic Religious Community. He did not hesitate to repress Arianism. He began to assert himself as the all-sufficient master of the political and ecclesiastical world that he ruled. He began a ruthless campaign to take back the Donation of Constantine by eliminating bishops, clergy and religious nonconformists from the Melchite and Exterior Coptic Religious Communities. Prior to the Council of Constantinople II, Justinian and his wife, Theodora, disposed of the African papa Agapetus I (535-536) who died a mysterious and sudden death in Constantinople and then disposed of Silverius (536-537), the next elected papa by the Melchite Coptic community who was accused of

Roman Emperor Justinian I (527-565 A.C.E.) was the builder of the world's first Christian church, the Hagia Sophia (532 A.C.E.). He became the world's first Roman Catholic Byzantine European pope with complete ecclesiastical authority after the Council of Constantinople II (553 A.C.E.). Shown here wearing a pope's miter fashioned after the Ancient Egyptian symbolic Crown of Jurisdiction.

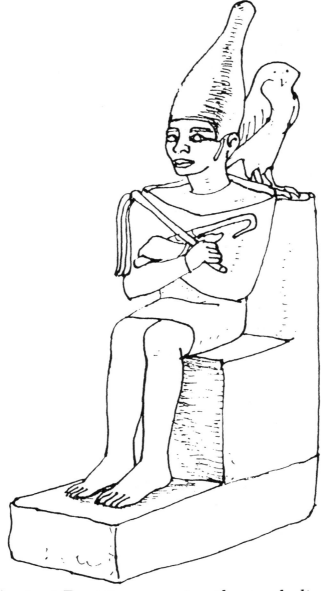

An Ancient Egyptian wearing the symbolic Crown of Jurisdiction.

treason. This was all being done because Justinian wanted ecclesiastical authority when he completed the building of the Hagia Sophia in 537. He also disposed of the world's first person to have the real authentic title of Pope of the Roman (Byzantine) Catholic Church, the Hagia Sophia, with ecclesiastical authority. That person was Vigilius (537–555). He was an African. Justinian disposed of Vigilius for not condemning the Three Nestorian Chapters and for not taking communion with the Monophysites. The reason Vigilius had objected to Justinian's interference in the affairs of the Coptic Religious Communities was on the grounds that Justinian's meddling went against the creed of the Donation of Constantine. For these and other reasons, Justinian disposed of Vigilius.

In this attitude, Justinian reflected the principle power of the Byzantine Imperial government. Ecclesiastical power outside of the emperor was now unthinkable. In the Christian context, he pushed this notion to its logical conclusion: since all power was from God (Osiris), then he, as the so-called Christian emperor, enjoyed the fullness of power by so-called "divine right." He was to exercise this "divine right" for the well-being of the Empire and spread this man-made occult religion called Christianity throughout the world with himself as leader, Pope and Vicar of Christ.

So, with imperial and ecclesiastical power over the Coptic Exterior Religious Community and the Melchite Religious Community in the hands of a Roman Byzantine ruler, Justinian I made himself, in essence, the world's first European Roman Catholic pope with full ecclesiastical authority thereby beginning the Roman Catholic papacy as Caesar-O Pope. He took full leadership of the Hagia Sophia, the world's first Christian and Roman Catholic Church, and began to establish monasteries and churches throughout Constantinople and parts of Rome. He also elected figure head powerless patriarchs from the African Dyophysitic Community such as Pelagius I (556–561) and John III (561–574) to sit in as the Bishop of the Hagia Sophia.

Thus far in today's Roman Catholic Church, only European white men have been elected pope (Bishop) of this spiritually dead world organization since moving to the Vatican in 1445. Consider all you have read in this book regarding the conquering Europeans and their influence and persuasion that helped develop the icon Serapis into the Christ. Also remember that the Greeks and Romans came to Egypt as pagans and heathens without any gods or spiritual awareness.   Bringing with them an agnostic, physical, brutal, uncivilized, savage life style, void of the knowledge of the creator. Again remember it was our Coptic Egyptian ancestors who created this icon/image of Serapis/Christ for the Europeans thereby helping the Romans to force this European spiritless icon/image upon us and the world. This, in turn, started our spiritual destruction and confusion. I urge you to turn within yourself and use the spirituality that your creator gave you at the time of your birth, thereby removing the need of a man-made religion.

Note, The Melchite African Copts also created within the Hagia Sophia the world's first academic institution for the Europeans. Within this institution, the entire faculty was Coptic Melchite African Egyptians thereby becoming the teachers of the Europeans in an organized institution. This institution, on the orders of Justinian and his wife, Theodora, only allowed young males to enroll who took the oath of celibacy. The curriculum and teachings of the Melchite Copts at this institution is the most likely source of any factual information that may be available to us today about the Ancient Egyptians of Antiquity. Some of this information is available today and can be found in the Coptic library and museum in the Vatican in Rome.

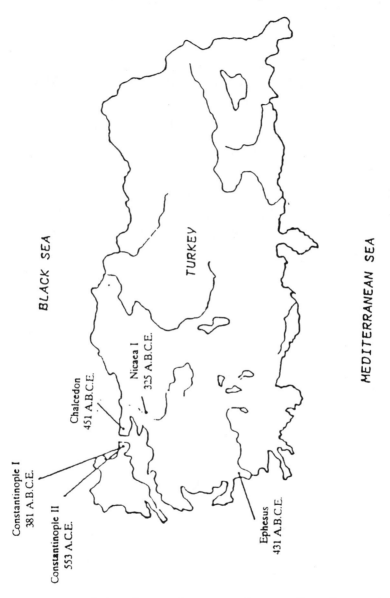

BLACK SEA

MEDITERRANEAN SEA

TURKEY

Nicaea I
325 A.B.C.E.

Chalcedon
451 A.B.C.E.

Constantinople I
381 A.B.C.E.

Constantinople II
553 A.C.E.

Ephesus
431 A.B.C.E.

This map of Turkey shows where the first five council meetings were held.

It should again be pointed out that Constantinople in Northeast Africa was the place where the Europeans received their civilization via the teaching institute of the Hagia Sophia and not in Greece.   To further substantiate this point, I reiterate (1) the Greeks had no alphabet prior to coming into contact with the Ancient Egyptians; and (2) the Greeks did not have any institutions in Greece during the time of antiquity. (See Chapters VIII and IX.)

CHAPTER VIII

THE HISTORICAL ORIGIN OF THE NAME JESUS

Before the Greeks and Romans, who are one and the same, entered Egypt, they had no God, goddess or gods. Nor did they have an alphabet. They were instead an agnostic, physical, psychopathic, illiterate, uncivilized European race of people who were not in-tune with the spiritual rhythm of the universe. After seeing what greatness the Ancient Egyptians had achieved with their in-tune spiritual universal consciousness, they wanted to become part of that great spiritual connection the Ancient Egyptians had with the Universal Creator, but with themselves being worshipped as a god. This is why Alexander the Greek and Ptolemy I Soter wanted so much to be accepted into the sacred priest society of Ancient Egypt (see Chapter I), which takes us to the time in history when the image and the name Serapis first came into being.

In this chapter, I will explain how the name "Jesus" first came into existence. This name came into being 1565 years after the image and name Serapis were created by the Melchite Coptic Egyptian priest society in Memphis, Egypt 320 B.C.E. (see Chapter I). This created Icon called Serapis was worshipped along with the Ancient Egyptian goddess, Isis, throughout Greece, Rome and the Byzantine Roman Empire. Serapis took the place of the Ancient Egyptian god, Osiris. This form of dual worship (Serapis and Isis) stayed in place in the Greek and Roman world until the Council of Ephesus (431 A.B.C.E.) (see Chapter V). During this council meeting, the created Icon of Serapis was made the Messias ([K]Christos-Christ) who went on to become the God and object of the Christian world. It was at this point that Isis was stripped of her attributes, discarded and replaced with the created creature, the Virgin Mary. Consequently, this left the Greeks in Greece and the Romans in Rome and the rest of the Europeans living under the Byzantine rule with just an icon with a title (Christ). An icon who could not be called Serapis any longer. However, the Greeks and Romans con-

Fig A. Zeus

Fig B. Jupiter
In Greek and Roman mythology, Zeus and Jupiter are one and the same god. Note the likeness of the icon Jesus.

tinued to worship this icon Christos (Christ) as their god by changing its name to Iezv, today pronounced "Zeus" for the Greeks and Iūpiter (Jupiter) for the Romans.

In Greek and Roman Mythology, Zeus and Jupiter are one and the same god. The derivative of the name Jesus is from the name Zeus, i.e., Iezv, or Iesū, as it is spelled today using the Greek-Latin alphabet. Always remember, the Greek and Latin alphabets are derivatives of the phonetic alphabet, which is the second form of writing of the Ancient Egyptians. (The first form of writing is called today Medu Netcher, i.e., hieroglyphic; the second is called today hieratic-demotic). Allow me to reiterate. The Greeks, prior to the coming of Alexander the Greek's invasion of Ancient Egypt in 332 B.C.E., had no alphabet. The Greeks were an illiterate people without an alphabet who were unable to read or write, thereby unable to record any data pertinent to their time and evolution as a people. Subsequently, Alexander forced the Greek language on the Ancient Egyptians, which caused them to apply an alphabet to the Greek language. This was the phonetic alphabet, that is sometimes identified as the phoenician alphabet which is a misnomer. The reason this is a misnomer is ... a Phoenician never existed on earth in human form. Phoenicians are fictitious characters used in narrative stories in written literature only. So again as one can see, the Greeks had no alphabet prior to entering Egypt in 332 B.C.E.

The name Iesūs was first applied to the icon, Christ during the first Ecumenical Council of Lyons in the year 1245 A.C.E. which is counted as the 13th Ecumenical Council. At this council, the Christians in Rome, Germany, and France banded together under the leadership of Innocent IV who had fled Rome to convoke a meeting in Lyons, France to deal with their struggle with the Ecclesiastical authority of the Holy Roman Emperor Frederick II over the Christian community under his rule and to adopt a first given name for the Christ Logos. This was done because the African and European Monophysite Community in Africa (1240 A.C.E.) had begun to use the biography and life of Ibn Al 'Arabi, alias Mohammed, as their object of their new forming religion which today is known as Muhammedanism/ Islam (See The Historical Origin of Islam by this Author). This left the Christ icon with only a title identity (Christ). At this point, the Christian fathers under the leadership of Innocent IV borrowing from the name *Zeus* came up with a first given name Iesūs for the Christ icon, thereby calling this icon "Iesūs the Christ." The Monophysites in keeping with their new Monophysite theology of the thirteenth century brought about the creation of a new religion called Muhammadism, later to be called Islam. This was done by the African and European Monophysites after fusing their Monophysitic Christian theology into the new name "Muhammed" thus making Muhammad to become Muhammad the Christ.

The following word diagram will show how this name (Jesus) progression was formulated. Remember there was no letter "J" in 1240 A.C.E. when the name Iesūs or Jesus was applied to the created icon, Christ.

"I" = Z: The letter "Z" originally had a strong resemblance to the symbol that we recognize today as the upper case or capital "I." See the alphabet chart on page 88. Compare lines 7 and 10. Although "Z" went through a visual transformation, "I" and "Z" were synonymous: Ieus, Zeus. The "I" eventually was adopted as the upper case of "i."

iesūs - Zeus: iesūs, the phonetic Greek and pre-renaissance spelling for the name Jesus. The "i" functioned as a vowel and consonant (j) prior to 1630 when "j" assumed the function of a consonant.

In the year 1630, the Europeans took the letter "i" and created a new letter for the Latin-English alphabet; that letter being the letter "j," which is explained in the following chapter. One should note that in the romance language, Spanish, the enunciation of the name Jesus is pronounced Hay-Zeus, but spelled "Jesus." Also, I would like to bring to your attention that the icon/image of Serapis/Christ has five different names applied to the same image and are as follows:
- Serapis
- Christ (today called Jesus the Christ)
- Zeus
- Jupiter
- Mohammed (the faceless icon of Islam who sometimes is given the same attributes as Christ, thereby, causing this faceless icon to be referred to as "Muhammad the Christ")

NOTE: Serapis, Christ, Zeus, and Jupiter are all called the Soter (Savior) sometimes spelled "Souter."

Christel   Muhammed

The two created creatures, Christ and the faceless Muhammad. Ibn Al 'Arabi became the faceless Muhammad in 1239–1240 A.C.E. There remains no known icons/images of Ibn Al 'Arabi, alias Muhammad, who later became the foundation of Islam.

CHAPTER IX

THE HISTORICAL ORIGIN OF THE LETTER "J"

It should be evident that "The Historical Origin of Christianity" has been written for numerous reasons. One of the primary purposes is to familiarize the populous with the historical cosmological realities of Christianity as opposed to the usual diet of traditions, myths and fables. Traditions and other teachings simply have been passed on to succeeding generations through the centuries. A great number of recipients of these teachings simply are not aware. For example, it was a group of Roman Catholic priests attending The Ecumenical Council of Trent called by the Roman Catholic Church, 1545-1563, who arbitrarily made key history affecting decisions that were artificial and would be passed on as "Truth." At this council meeting, a group of "church leaders" led by the pope resolved that certain writtings would be considered inerrant, infallible, and the word of God, i.e., the New Testament! (This action was taken because Martin Luther after starting the Protestant Movement against the Roman Catholic Church, 1517, began teaching his Protestant Christians in 1535 that the Old Testiment, Bible printed for the first time in 1475 A.C.E. was devine, canonical and genuine. Additionally, Luther taught that the New Testament was apocrypha, noncanonical pseudepigrapha writings that were first propounded by his contemporary Desederius Erasmus in 1516. To counter this charge, the Roman Catholic Church at the Council of Trent, 1546 made claims that the Novum Instrumentum or New Testament commissioned by Pope Alexander VI in 1500, written and subsequently completed by Erasmus in 1516 was indeed infallible, without error, and indeed, the word of God. From that time, forward, they effectively ensured that the questioning and inquisitions surrounding the authorship of this pseudepigrapha apocrypha literature would be minimized. This is a strking example of how an outgrowth of tradition and arbitrary decision making by a few yesterday is accepted as fact and truth today. Unfortunately, with the passage of time, true history is forgotten or lost and another contrived history emerges.

Because of this confusion, thousands of men and women within and without the walls of academia have devoted and wasted their lives trying to substantiate and give historicity to the traditons, myths and fables that abound in religious literature incluidng the Torah, the Bible, and the Koran respectively.   Another excellent example is presented in Chapter V which also validates this point.   Chapter V illustrates how the images of the creature, Serapis/Christ, and its created mother, the Virgin Mary, were both fabricated.   Both creatures were man-made and now many years later with the passage of time they are presented to the world as human beings who once lived.

My brothers and sisters who embrace Judaism and Islam should not take comfort, for the prophets of the old testament were created by way of perki avot pseudepigraphous literature.   And the faceless Prophet of Islam and its given name Muhammed were devised through a compromise by the Monophysite Christians.   Muhammed is the same created creature as Serapis/Christ, but without a face and no human nature.   Remember that the original Monophysites accepted that Serapis had an Osiris-like spirit and no human nature.   Thus came the split and renaming of the Christ image to the created name Mohammed (1240 A.C.E.).   Further, the authority of the Torah and Koran was created and institutionalized through a process similar to that undergone by the New Testament. Innocently, most of us are led to step inside a religion and accept the literature of that religion by faith, without questioning the origin of either. Once inside, the indoctrination is set in motion seldom to be interrupted. We submit consciously and unconsciously. Our spiritual energy then is utilized to sustain the myths, untruths, and perpetuate traditions.

This chapter does not venture into the depths of various religious literature; however, readers are encouraged to step outside of all religions, religious literature and any other literature and question the very foundation of the institutions responsible for creating, housing, and disseminating such literature. Moreover, question who were the players who wrote the literature, when was it written, what was the motive, how and when, by whom was it actually documented, why so many variations and what are the original meanings of words and names? The Bible is not exempt - how, when, and by whom were the new and old testaments written? When were both testaments placed under one cover? What are the bases of the stories? Were the stories written by playwrights and poets such as Desederius Erasmus, Shakespeare, or Goethe? Why is the King James Bible considered the most important version? Who was King James? Moreover, should I simply accept by faith or facts which are verifiable by objective research that extends beyond Biblical, Torah or Koran literature? The definition of faith may be helpful in answering the latter question. According to Webster, faith is unquestionable belief. Faith encourages one not to question. In religion, adherents often are taught to feel guilty or a sense of failure if questions are raised. Has your faith, your religion, or the fear that runs subtlety through most religions intimidated you into silence and blind acceptance?

Fortunately, not all are intimidated into silence or blind acceptance. It is because one dared to raise questions and another accepted the challenge and responded to the questions by way of research that this chapter has been written. It is important to acknowledge that many today are sharing, questioning, and asking the not so obvious and difficult questions along with attending lectures.

Just as this chapter encourages one to question, please apply the same principle to this work. It is crucial that we all remain open to new information, the professionals as well as the lay. We must get back to the basic inquisitive type of questions such as who, what, when, where, how and why when receiving new information or reevaluating our existing bank of knowledge. None can afford not to question or merely blindly accept whatever we are told at face value. Therefore, it is imperative that we scrutinize, peruse, question and use our Creator-given ability to discern and ascertain what is reasonable, rationale and factual information. We must reclaim our innocence.

One of the many observations that has been presented frequently by audiences when Professor Williams lectures is the fact that the letter "j" is a relatively new addition to the English alphabet along with the reasonable assumption that the created Christ of Christianity must have had a name other than Jesus. Given the above, initially some have assumed that this book is solely about the "name Jesus." Undoubtedly, by now the reader realizes that this is not the case after reading the preceding chapters. However, because this supposition surfaced repeatedly, research was warranted.

Included in this chapter are a brief overview of the history of the alphabet and a specific discussion of the letter "j" and related letters. Have you given any thought to the origin of the alphabet or the letters that comprise the alphabet?

First, a definition of alphabet: alphabet is the name given to a set of graphic signs, called letters, denoting elementary sounds, by the combination of which words can be visibly represented.

As with so many treasures from Africa that have been renamed, relabeled or stolen, the alphabet is no exception. It is important to be aware that every alphabet of the civilized world has evolved from one of the three scripts of the Ancient Egyptians, i.e., hieroglyphics, hieratic-demotic or cursive and phonetic. PERHAPS ONE OF THE GREATEST ACHIEVEMENTS OF THE ANCIENT EGYPTIANS WAS THE WORKING OUT OF THE FIRST SYSTEM OF WRITING (see chart on the following page). The adapted Roman/Latin alphabet that is widely used today has only been on the scene of history since the European Renaissance.

Some scholars have promulgated the false notion that the Roman/Latin alphabet was derived from the Greek. However, as previously stated in Chapter VIII, further investigation establishes that the so-called Greek alphabet is a misnomer and is actually the phonetic alphabet created by the Ancient Egyptians. This phonetic alphabet was applied to the Greek language by the Coptic Egyptian scholars speaking Greek. The Greeks did not have an alphabet. Prior to the Greek invasion of Ancient Egypt, the Greeks did not read or write and definitely had not developed a civilization of which writing is considered an integral part.

	EGYPTIAN			GREEK				LATIN		
1	𓅭	2	ᴧ	A	A	ᴧ	a	A	A	ᴧaa
2	𓅯	⚡	ϟ	8	B	B	β	β	B	B b
3	▱	Z	7	1	Γ	Γ	⌐Y	<	C	{C GcGG}
4	⌒	ᴧ	Δ	Δ	Δ	ᴧ	δ	D	D	ᴧ ᴧ d
5	⊓	m	Ⅎ	Ⅎ	E	E	ε	℉	E	e e
6	⟿	⟋	ⴹ	ⴹ	YF		f	F	F	ᒋf
7	🦂	ℓ	‡	‡	I	Z	ZC	‡	Z	z
8	●	⌒	⊟	⊟	H	H	h η	⊟	H	h h
9	⊂⊃	⟾	⊕	⊕	⊙	⊖	ϑ ϑ	⊗		
10	∖∖	𝘺	𝟤	⟨	l	l	ι	l	l	i j
11	⌒	⟍	𝟺	Ⅎ	K	K	κ κ	K	K	k
12	⟿	ℓ	ℓ	V	Λ	λ	λ	ʟ	L	l l
13	🐂	3	𝟽	M	M	M	μ μ	ᴦᴦ	M	m m
14	〜	⟍	𝟺	ᴎ	N	N	ν ν	ᴎ	N	n n
15	→	→	‡	‡	Ξ	Ȝ	Ɛ	⊞	+	x x
16			o	o	O	O	o	O		
17	⊞	𝟺	⟩	⟩	Γ	π	π ϖ	P	P	P
18	⟋	⟋	ᴦ	ᴦ	M		ᴀ	ᴦ		
19	◿	⟲	φ	φ	φ	ϙ		φ	Q	q q
20	⌒	⟍	⟨	⟨	P	P	ϙ P	ϼ	R	ᴩ r
21	⏟	⟋	w	⟩	⟨	C	⊂ σ	⟨	S	ʃ ʃ s
22	⟩	ᕼ	‡	⊤	T	T	τ	T	T	τ t
	i	ii	iii	iv	v	vi	vii	viii	ix	x

The Alphabet Chart

Showing the world's first system of writing by the Ancient Egyptians: the hieroglyphic, hieratic-demotic and the phonetic. From the phonetic Ancient Egyptian alphabet came the Greek/Latin alphabets.

The Ancient Egyptians, in contrast to the Greeks, were a literate people. They traveled around the world and applied their phonetic alphabet to the sound of the language spoken by the people with whom they came in contact. This adaptability is one of the outstanding characteristics of the phonetic alphabet.

Not only are the Greek, Latin and phonetic scripts one and the same, the Coptic script is included. As you are probably aware, Copt or Coptic means a direct descendant of the Ancient Egyptians. What is now called the Arabic script, another misnomer, is the hieratic-demotic script, the supposed cursive form of writing which is the second form of writing of the Ancient Egyptians written today in calligraphy with modern adaptations. Further, it is important to note that the Ancient Egyptians during the time of antiquity were the only people who were literate. The rest of the world was illiterate, including the Greeks and the Romans.

I will proceed with a discussion of the letter "j." It is a known historical fact that the letter "j" did not exist during the creation of the image Serapis/Christ (320 B.C.E.) or during the time that the Serapis/Christ image was given a pseudo human nature at the Council of Ephesus (431 A.B.C.E.).

The letter "j" was "developed" or perhaps more appropriately fully evolved and came into prominence in the seventeenth century, the year 1630 A.C.E. This was during the latter part of the European Renaissance when the masses of Europe were just beginning to be taught to read and write. Prior to this period, reading and writing were reserved for young hand-picked males who were a part of the Hagia Sophia. Later, the Roman Catholic Monastery School system trained males to become priests/teachers and taught the rich monarchs and merchants of Europe who could afford to hire private tutors for their families. Note, it was the Coptic African Egyptians who established the first educational institution for Europeans which began in the Hagia Sophia, the world's first Christian church built in 532 A.C.E., located in Constantinople (modern Istanbul), Turkey (see pages 61-64).

The letter "j" had its genesis in the letter "i" which appears to have had its origin in the third writing form of the Ancient Egyptians, the phonetic. Today the phonetic alphabet is often classified under the misnomers of phoenician or early Greek, Latin or old Hebrew. It is important to our understanding when studying the alphabet to know that every alphabet had its beginning in Ancient Egypt. Remember, the Ancient Egyptians developed the first form and system of writing.

The alphabet has undergone numerous changes such as additions, deletions, order, sound, definitions, variations in appearance, accidents, and sometimes usage, confluence, and function.

Dualism has characterized several letters such as "v" which also served the function of "u" before its introduction into the alphabet. Relevant to this discussion, the letter "i" prior to 1630 was used as a vowel and a consonant. According to those who study the origin of languages, to distinguish its use as a vowel and consonant, the "i" was placed above the line to represent a vowel and below the line to identify it as a consonant. Additionally, "i" was considered a calligraphic variation standing for consonant "y." On this same point, the Britannica World Dictionary states that "j" was originally identified with the Roman "I" and in the seventeenth century, the calligraphic practice of carrying the "i" which usually had consonant value both above and below the line. The "i" gradually developed into a graphic distinction between the vowel "i" and "j" the consonant. Webster's Collegiate Dictionary also confirms that the form and function gradually became differentiated.

Therefore, it seems logical to conclude that the "j" is etymologically closely related to "i," "y," considering its sound, "g" and "z" as well.

Scholars, such as Frederick Goudy, indicate that both "i's" had the same sound whether used as a vowel or consonant, while others indicate that "i" had a number of sounds. The sound of "j" as we know it today was adopted into the English language from the French language and is pronounced in French as "zh," "u" and "zu." In English, "j" possesses the sound of the "g" in genius. The French "j" has evolved into a different sound as we can see in French words that have been retained in the English language, e.g., jabot, bijou.

As we further explore, more information emerges to stimulate the left side of our brain, the center of reasoning and analyzing. The letters "i" and "j" are more than alphabets. "I" is a prefix of obscuring meaning. Another consideration is one we are all familiar with, "i" a normative case of the pronoun by which a person denotes him- or herself. In French, the pronoun "je" translates into the English pronoun "I." In French, "je" never stands alone. Interestingly, it is connected to an action verb and then combined and written as one word.

Given this nuance of French, one is left to speculate or ask whether the "je" ("i") is an affix or add on to "sus" (pronounced zoos or zeus), producing Jesus.   In Chapter VIII, Professor Williams gave the Spanish/Phonetic spelling, Hay-Zesus.   French and Spanish are both romance languages, similar in structure, function and sound. Ponder this information and possibilities and draw your own conclusions.

Even after the distinction in writing was made, the feeling persisted that "i" and "j" were one and the same continued into the nineteenth century. Words in the dictionary beginning with "i" and "j" were listed together.   One can go to almost any library and page through old dictionaries or indexes of publications printed in the 1800s and early 1900s and observe the correlation.   Because the "i" and "j" were considered synonymous, would it be safe for one to conclude that the pronunciations or sounds matched?

Reference the Alphabet Chart on page 88). This table shows how the Phonetic letters passed through Greek and Latin forms to reach their present English forms.

A number of letters in the chart are germane to our discussion of the name of Jesus, particularly the letter that appears similar to capital "I" which has its origin in the Phonetic alphabet and eventually became the letter "z" (line seven of Alphabet Chart). Then "z" was removed altogether and later restored, not to the seventh position in the alphabet, but to the 23rd, and later to the 26th position subsequent to the addition of the letters "j," "u" and "w." Today, "j" is the tenth letter in the alphabet following "i." However, in the printer's "upper case" on the press, the capital letters are arranged alphabetically, but "j" and "u" still come after "z," perhaps, owing to the unwillingness of the printers to change their presses probably for economic reasons. Moreover, perhaps the arrangement bears witness to the evolution of the alphabet.

On line seven of the Alphabet Chart, going back to the Ancient Egyptian phonetic section, observe the symbol that closely resembles what we know today as the capital letter "I." As you follow across from left to right, you will see "I" come to look like the letter "z" under the Greek. Under early Latin "z" reappeared as "i" and during later Latin, "I" became "z" again. One author showed "I" all the way across his particular chart, disappearing under Latin altogether and reappearing under the English as "z." While the appearance varied, it is most probable that the function and sound remained consistent.

To further enhance your understanding of Chapter VIII, it is essential that we single out "z" as an important letter of the alphabet in our discussion as it relates to the origin of the name Jesus (Iesus). "Z," as most letters in our alphabet, had its beginning in Ancient Egypt, as mentioned earlier. The letter "z" is considered etymologically most closely related to "s," "y," "j" and "i." In other words, they are considered cognate or related letters which means that they are commutable into each other, interchangeable in many instances, passing regularly into each other and possessing the same fundamental idea. For example, study the names visually: Zesus, Iesus, Jesus, Sesus, Yesus.

Walter Whiter expounds on this concept of commutability in his text, "Universal Etymological Dictionary." He states that consonants alone are to be regarded in discovering the affinity of words and that vowels are to be wholly rejected because they afford no principle of uniformity or laws of distinction, but add variability and confusion. Whiter divided consonants into three classes after the following manner:

1. M,B,F,P,V
2. C,D,G,J,K,Q,S,T,X,Z
3. L,N,R

A review of the consonants that comprise class two (2) clearly supports the premise that there is an etymological relationship between the various names and titles given to the image known today as Jesus the Christ, i.e., Serapis (savior), Christ, Iesūs (Jesus), Zeus and Iūpiter (Jupiter).

One should remember that words and names have contended with amalgamation or fusion. An excellent example of amalgamation can be referenced in Chapter I regarding how the name Serapis, which was Osirapis before modification, was formulated by combining the name of the god Osiris with the name of the sacred bull Apis, thus the process of the amalgamation of a name. Amalgamation is akin to the process of Theocrasia. The Coptic Egyptians, in their attempt to appease the Greek Ptolemy, developed the process of Theocrasia by taking the attributes of their two gods, Osiris and Apis, and merged them, hence [O]Serapis, today called Jesus or Zeus and Iesūs prior to the introduction of the letter "J" during the seventeenth century.

Words and names also have contended with translations, interpretation, transliterations, transpositions, accidents, confluences, regionalization, time and the respelling of words during the Renaissance era. As previously mentioned, many words and names which contain the letter "j" were initially spelled with the letter "i," such as Iulius before Julius, Iesuits preceded Jesuits, Iūpiter before Jupiter, Iack for Jack, and Iesūs predates Jesus.

It could be said that the letter "j" eased its way into the English alphabet as a consonant, first as an "i" written below the line to denote its use as a consonant and later a curve was added to the bottom of the letter to further distinguish either deliberately or by a quirk of the hand.

"I" and "i" have been used throughout this chapter. Given how we use them today, it is easy to think of them as being upper case and lower case respectively. The concept of upper and lower case is a late development and did not exist in the early history of the alphabet. That which can seem so fundamental in the current state does not necessarily indicate that it has always been. Names and words are relevant in the time and geographical location in which they are devised and used. This is especially true of popular names. Original names, spellings, and pronunciations are retained locally most likely if they are popular, even in the face of apparent changes later in pronunciation or spelling elsewhere.

As stated earlier in this chapter, it was the Coptic Egyptians who established the first educational institution for the Europeans in the first Christian church, the Hagia Sophia in 537 A.C.E.

School and church have continued as one and the same through the centuries and even today. The Roman Catholic and Protestant churches created the European renaissance era by building schools to educate the masses in the secular community during the sixteenth century. The influence of religion and the role of the church school curriculums become obvious in the creation of words, names, definitions, and usage.

Arnetta May
Instructor – The Ancient Egyptian Institute
Member – The Ancient Egyptian Research Society
Member – The Society of New Scholars (SUNS)
Chicago, Illinois

CHAPTER X

CONCLUDING COMMENTS

This book is written to set you spiritually free of all religious bondage that our Melchite Coptic Egyptian ancestors unwittingly helped to set into motion Christianity, Islam, and Judaism. Western society uses these religions as political tools to indoctrinate the world masses. This includes your great grandparents, your grandparents, your parents, and now you.

Any person reading this book should by now know that I confirm my heritage as an Ancient Egyptian. I will spend the rest of my life sharing my research with those oppressed descendants of the original Ancient Egyptians among us who will find their own way back as they resurrect the spiritual consciousness of Ancient Egypt within them.

Many times after giving a lecture on the historical origin of Christianity, I am asked the question, "If what you say is true and there has never been a man that walked the earth in human form of any race, creed or color by the name of Jesus Christ, then what do I put in its place?" My answer is, you were born with a Divine Spiritual Birthright and that Divine Spiritual Birthright was given to you at the time of your birth by the She/He Creator who used your mother and father as human instruments to bring you forth in human form. This Divine Spiritual Birthright is your life spirit that dwells inside of you at this very moment. At the time of your birth, your divine in-dwelling spirit or spirituality was connected to, and spiritually in tune with, the spiritual consciousness and rhythm of the universe through your pineal gland brain fibers which are connected to your nostrils, taking in the air that you breathe. The air you breathe keeps you in spiritual consciousness with your creator and the spiritual rhythm of the universe thereby giving you a personal relationship with your creator. I have been fortunate not to allow any man-made religion to sever or confuse my personal relationship with my Creator. You were born with the same birthright. Use it. Always remember that you were born spiritually free of all man-made religions, i.e., no one was born with a religion. What happened is that man-made religion was introduced to confuse the natural spiritual cosmic unity you have with the She/He Creator. In its place, you were indoctrinated by man in one of his man-made/pagan/heathen/occult religions, such as Christianity, Islam, Black Hebraism, Judaism, Buddhism, etc. These religions were designed for political and social control. By not understanding your natural spiritual connection with your Creator, you allowed man to confuse and substitute your naturally given spiritual birthright with one of his man-made unnatural religions. This is similar to being introduced to cigarettes, alcohol, or drugs. You were not born with cigarettes, alcohol, or drugs, nor were you born with any of the man-made religions. Man-made religions, cigarette smoking, drinking alcohol and the using of drugs are all man-introduced.

Always remember, your Creator provided you with all of your spiritual needs at the time of your birth. The introduction of religion was done to place governments, nations, and all of the civilized world under the control of an assortment of man-organized religions. One must always remember that all religions today are used as political tools of control. Political, military, economic (including taxation) and social control have proven to be easier under man-made religious rulership. This was also the smoothest path for eventual world domination and the acquisition of absolute power, misdistribution of wealth, and a world population of obedient, religious slaves.

Always remember, our ancestors, the Ancient Egyptians, never had or practiced a religion. They practiced what is called today the "Maathian Creed," a natural spiritual way of life that was in tune with the spiritual consciousness and rhythm of the universe based on the cosmic natural laws of Maat (truth, justice, peace, wisdom, and love). The icon Serapis was introduced for a political purpose: that purpose was to get our Coptic Egyptian ancestors to worship and apotheosize a European icon as God. This eventually happened over many years, starting with the Dyophysitic Coptic Egyptian Christians who began to worship this European spiritless icon called Serapis under the new name and title, Christ. This laid the foundation for Christianity, for the Roman Byzantine Catholic Church the Hagia Sophia, and the entire world.

The information written in this book is very vital to our African community at this time in world history. If we are to advance out of this mental and spiritual confusion, we must have the knowledge of what happened to our Ancient Egyptian ancestors in the past, in order for us to know what has to be done in the future. If I had not written this book, chances are you would never have known the true historical origin of Christianity, because Christian theology (as taught throughout history today) will never reveal this to you. The reason is that the European religious and academic communities have erased the Coptic Egyptian origin of Christianity thereby creating a total European (i.e., racist) world view of Christianity. This is done by getting you to believe that God so loved the world that he sent his only begotten son, Jesus the Christ, to save the world from sin. This is teaching you, the believer, to believe that God's only begotten son is European with long flowing blond hair, blue eyes and a heavy facial beard (i.e., giving the illusion that the European is the embodiment of god on earth in the form of the incarnated Jesus the Christ). At this point, you are encouraged to embrace this European image as your personal savior and god. This starts you to subconsciously act docile in the presence of Europeans which gives them the illusion that they should think, act and feel superior over people of African descent and other races of color.

Since we as a people of African descent have been spiritually disconnected from our Ancient Egyptian ancestors, we do not think and live our lives as subjects of our own ancestral historical experience. Therefore, we conduct our lives based on illusions set in place for us by the European society through their educational and religious systems. For instance, the three major religions such as Christianity, Islam, and Judaism teach the descendants of the Ancient Egyptians to hate their ancestors, culture, and civilization by teaching through sermon and religious literature that the Ancient Egyptians were evil and disobeyed the laws of God thereby bringing about their own destruction. Our lives and experiences are based on these European-created illusions. These illusions create confusion and disorder in our everyday thinking. Being spiritually and consciously aware of the greatness of our Ancient Egyptian ancestors' history and culture will help to dispel these illusions and myths.

One has to realize that the European value system that we live under teaches us European traditions and purposely lead the descendants of Ancient Egypt away from Ancient Egyptian thought and culture. Europeans have long been working on changing the spiritual nature of us as a people. They began with our Ancient Egyptian ancestors, starting with the entrance of Alexander the Greek in Egypt in 332 B.C.E. The descendants of these Europeans continue to this very day to mislead the descendants of the Ancient Egyptian people whom they have trained to call themselves Nubians, Sudanese, Ethiopian, Negro, Black, and now African-American. This has been done by remapping the world, slavery and by their organized educational and religious system. Ironically, while the Europeans were teaching and steering the descendants of the Ancient Egyptians away from the knowledge and truth of their ancestors, they began to engage in a monumental effort to take control and distort the truth about Ancient Egypt and the Ancient Egyptians. One of their first tactics was to take Ancient Egypt away from its African origin and identity. With cunning intent, this was accomplished through word manipulation and semantics. Attempts were made to remove Egypt from the continent of Africa and place it in a nonexistent Middle East. Today, the European academic community has devised a vicious and devious scheme to make the Ancient Egyptians appear to be Europeans by portraying

Ptolemaic and Roman Egypt before the eyes of the world masses. A second tactic used to gain control of Ancient Egypt is their claim to have deciphered the Medu-Netcher or hieroglyphics. Their claim is based on the supposed finding of the Rosetta Stone, the Stone of Canopus, Champollion and Adolph Erman who published in 1880 the world's first supposed grammatical dictionary of the hieroglyphs, and the works of others. (See Appendix for the repudiation of the decipherment of the hieroglyphics, page 146).

I will now quote Carter G. Woodson, the author of *The Mis-Education of the Negro*, "our religious and education systems have justified slavery, peonage, lynching, segregation, discrimination and mass arrest of African-American people. If you can control a man's thinking you do not have to worry about his actions." These words are as true today as they were when written in 1933.

I now conclude by sharing with you what I was told many years ago about the word "facts." Facts, I was told, are stronger than argument, more profound than reasoning, more dependable than opinions, silences dispute, supersedes predictions, and facts always end the argument.

I HAVE DONE MY DUTY BY PUTTING THE FACTS IN WRITING. NOW YOU MUST JUDGE FOR YOURSELF.

Walter Williams
Historian and Research Analyst
of Ancient History and Related Subjects

Founder of

THE ANCIENT EGYPTIAN MUSEUM

THE ANCIENT EGYPTIAN INSTITUTE

THE ANCIENT EGYPTIAN
RESEARCH SOCIETY

THE SOCIETY OF NEW SCHOLARS (SUNS)

Chicago, Illinois

SUMMARY

This book is a departure from the norm of scholarly research. The *Historical Origin of Christianity* is small in size, but big on information. The author gets directly to the point in this, his first of many undertakings. No longer must we labor with the wordiness and excessive posturing that is done with many books of this nature. The scholarly community has always equated volume with superiority or wisdom. Quantity does not always mean quality. We as a people have to get out of the notion of being impressed and look to be informed. In James Henry Breasted's book, *A History of Egypt*, he expounds for some 600 pages on a subject he knew little about. He even told us so in his preface and later apologized to his readers. Why didn't he just tell us what he did know? The reason is that his book would probably be no greater in volume than this author's work. Instead, he uses inference, conjecture, fragments, and outright untruths to write his version of the history of Egypt. Walter Williams has avoided this. From the very opening of Chapter I, you are taken directly to the "meat" of his subject. The author has an aversion to wasting space and time. His objective is to get you to see that it was your ancestors, the Coptic Egyptians, who created the icon/image of Serapis/Christ which was done for the purpose of political control.

The Historical Origin of Christianity is a fine piece of investigative research. Walter Williams has analyzed the evidence and will challenge your traditional views about Christianity. Here is a scholar who has boldly stepped outside of the norm. He has accomplished a feat no other person, or scholar for that matter, of biblical criticism has achieved. He has bypassed all of the biblical events (except to repudiate or to establish their true origin), to bring you an accurate origin of Christianity.

The Historical Origin of Christianity has brought forth "New Scholarship" to challenge Western Civilization at its foundation. This New Scholarship will challenge a primary cornerstone of Western Civilization— its religious institutions which have a strangle hold on the free thinking and, thus, the free will, of not only our people, but a majority of the people throughout the world.

Contrary to Christian doctrine, Walter Williams has told us that it was the Melchite Coptic

Egyptians who were the first Christians. If one doubts this, one should ask the question, if the Melchite Coptic Egyptians were not your first Christians, how is it that they took to it so well? I phrase this question on a historical basis, not a biblical one. The Melchite Coptic Egyptians had their own spiritual system in place. Their ancestors' culture had miraculously built the Great Pyramids—an accomplishment of which is only theorized today considering the then known technology. They also built the Great Sphinx and created three of the world's first alphabets. What could Christianity offer such a culturally and spiritually rich people as these? Has a Christian built a pyramid or a Temple of Karnak or Luxor? Has a Christian been able to mummify and preserve a corpse for over 3,000 years? Could being a Christian equal any of the past feats accomplished by the Ancient Egyptians? The answer is no! Then ask yourself: why would they need this new religion? Why weren't the Greeks and Romans your first community of Christians or some of the other pseudo-historical names such as the Babylonians, the Sumerians, the Persians, or even the Jews? The answer to these questions lie simply in the fact that the Melchite Coptic Egyptians were the first Christians because they created the image known today as Jesus. The Greeks and later the Romans turned the tables on these creators of Christianity and persuaded them through trickery to worship the icon of Serapis thereby completing the destruction of a great people! Walter Williams has written this book to bring forth this information and thus a New Scholarship!

In Chapter I, you were told how the image today called Jesus Christ, then known as Serapis, got the title of "Savior" applied to its name. In Chapter I, you were also told how the attributes of Osiris were linked with Serapis. You were then told when the image was first made; that there was a devious plot behind it. That devious plot was to get the Exterior Coptic Religious Community to worship Serapis, either directly as they tried to do during the Decian and Diocletian persecutions of the mid-third century and early fourth century A.B.C.E., or indirectly through what history is calling the "Donation of Constantine." The Donation of Constantine dealt the second destructive blow to the Coptic Egyptians' "Divine Spiritual Birthright." The first destructive blow came about when the person and icon of Ptolemy I, Lagi was given the assimilated characteristics of

Osiris and the name Serapis. Neither the Greeks nor the Romans had any notion of nor practiced a spiritual way of life. The Greeks and Romans only knew savagery and barbarism. This was a way of life for them. The Greeks and Romans in those times thought that the only way to subdue an enemy was to club, murder, maim, or bludgeon him into submission. They observed, however, that whatever it was that the Coptic Egyptians practiced, it made them peaceful, docile, orderly, obedient, passive, and revering. All of this without a single drop of blood being shed.

Alexander and the Ptolemies became aware of the spirituality of the Ancient Egyptians when they sat on the throne of Egypt and discovered that the people did not worship the Pharaoh. The Ancient Egyptians worshipped the unseen universal spiritual consciousness. The Greeks and Romans wanted to be a part of that worship, but with themselves being the worshipped. The Pharaoh's role was that of a CEO or president. He was the person responsible for keeping "Cosmic Order" or "Cosmic Balance." The Ancient Egyptians no more worshipped the Pharaoh than we worship the President of the United States today. The Pharaoh, buried in grand splendor, is the same as the president buried with "pomp and circumstance," a "twenty-one gun salute," or a "hail to the chief." To an alien culture, this would look like a form of worship. To worship out of fear is really not worship at all, it is fear. To worship someone out of respect, love and humility is the highest tribute that a human being can give. The Coptic Egyptians reserved this sort of worship only for the Creator, not for human flesh. Alexander and the Ptolemies wanted for themselves this honor that was reserved for the Creator.

In Chapter II, Walter Williams addresses the fallacy of the "Edict of Milan." There never was an Edict of Milan. The Edict of Milan was an insertion in history to veil the importance of the Donation of Constantine. As a matter of fact, at one time in history, the Donation of Constantine was used as the basis for ecclesiastical authority. Today, according to Lorenzo Valla, Nicholas of Cusa and Caesar Baronius, the Donation of Constantine is purported to be a fake and a forgery. Walter Williams does not believe this. It fits right into place with what happened beforehand with Donatism, and with what happened after the Donation of Constantine with "the strong statement by Arius."

There is no historical evidence of an Edict of Milan being issued by Emperor Constantine! Remember the persecutions I mentioned earlier (Decian and Diocletian)? Well, history is saying that Christians were being persecuted during these campaigns. Historically, there were no Christians during this era. Walter Williams has unveiled that it was our Ancient Egyptian Ancestors, the Coptic Egyptians, who were being persecuted by the Romans. Constantine's "edict" would have been issued to stop the persecution of the Exterior Coptic Religious Community which was already divided and weakened by the Donatist Schismatic Controversy. Instead of Constantine issuing an edict, he introduced the Donation of Constantine to this community.

The author has a message and it is simple: Give back the religion called Christianity to the people it was created for! This religion was created for Europeans to give them the appearance of being in tune with the spiritual rhythm of the universe. Let them reclaim it for themselves and allow the descendants of the Ancient Egyptians to recapture their natural spiritual connection with the Creator.

"If you don't have any knowledge of ancient history, you won't understand anything about religion," is what Walter frequently says. Ask yourself: Why were all the Roman emperors baptized, starting with Constantine? Why did all the persecutions stop after the Donation of Constantine? It is also clear that once the "Nicene Creed" was adopted, Theodosius tried to force the so-called Arianist to accept this creed. Just think, why would an emperor suffer public humiliation at the hands of a mere bishop? Why was "The Donation" given to Sylvester I and not the supposed pope of that day?

If we do not question history as it is popularly written, we only learn what the writers of history want us to know. If we spend the time and effort to do our own investigation, we might reach different conclusions, conclusions based upon facts previously unrevealed to you in traditional religious writings. If we don't learn to sort out fact from fiction, we will never be in control of our own destiny. Walter Williams has given us the key to unlock previously concealed information, information that will help us to reclaim our greatness as a people. It is up to us to recognize the value of what he is telling us. This is why investigative research is so important and valuable.

When you read about these council meetings in today's encyclopedias, you will not read anything about the Coptic Egyptians. So what happened to the world's first civilized people? What happened to their descendants? What happened to their culture? The descendants of the Ancient Egyptians are spread throughout the world calling themselves Nubians, Sudanese and Ethiopians, and a large population of their descendants are here in North America under the false and non-ethnic names of Negroes, Blacks and African-Americans. (This position will be brought out and dealt with more fully in a later publication.) With respect to the culture of the Ancient Egyptians, it, too, is spread throughout the entire world. The major players throughout the formation of Christianity were the Coptic Egyptians. The Melchites were Copts. Bishop Donatus and Bishop Secundus were Copts. Mensurius and Bishop Felix were Copts. Papa Sylvester I and also Theophilus were Coptic Egyptians. Just because they were Coptic Egypt-ians does not necessarily mean that they all were "credits to their race." Walter Williams likens the Melchites to the "Uncle Toms" of today. Indeed, they were the ones who created and apotheosized the image today called Jesus Christ after acquiescing to the wishes of the invaders. Arius, who was part of the resistance movement against Serapis, was loyal to the masses of Coptic Egyptians, and so was Donatus. Bishops Ambrose and Alexander were Melchites, but not necessarily devious Melchites, just misguided. Two examples of traitorous Melchite Coptic Egyptians are Sylvester I and Theophilus of Alexandria. Sylvester I was disloyal for accepting the Donation of Constantine and trying to get Serapis accepted into our ancestor's puritan spiritual community. Theophilus was disloyal for burning down the Serapeum Temple and annex building/library with the encouragement of Theodosius I. Theophilus did it to pave the way for the coming of Christianity.

Chapter V told us about the most important council meeting concerning the Serapis icon/image. This was where Serapis was transformed into the Messias-(K)Christos. Walter Williams was lured to these discoveries as he followed the image of Serapis. He also followed the one race, the one culture and the world's first and oldest civilized people, the Ancient Egyptians. Suffice it to say, to discuss the historical origins of Christianity without mentioning the Ancient Egyptians or the Coptic Egyptians is like trying to row upstream in a boat without a paddle.

The Council of Ephesus is when we can historically say Christianity began. The author is truly bringing forth New Scholarship in this chapter of the book. The Council of Ephesus is such a complex and intricate council meeting that most will miss its true significance with only a cursory reading. This council meeting was caused to come about by an Arianist faction called the Monophysites. The Monophysites emerged after the Council of Niceae I. These Coptic Egyptians were called Monophysites because they only recognized the divine Osiris-like characteristics in Serapis, but could not accept Serapis as God. Nestorius was a Monophysite and he challenged the dyophysitic union of the concocted Virgin-Theotokos (Mary) with the Incarnated Logos (Serapis). If we study the characteristics of the contrived Virgin Mary and study the title Theotokos and then compare it with the Ancient Egyptian Goddess, Isis, you will find the very same attributes (see illustration on page 52). Isis was called the Queen of Heaven and known as the Virgin Mother in Ancient Egyptian culture. The

Virgin Mary was also given the title Virgin Mother. Isis was depicted as a mother with her "sun" on her lap nursing her breast. The Virgin Mary is shown as a woman holding her son in her arms and some depictions show her holding her son on her lap. Isis was called the Mother of god (Horus). The Virgin Mary was given the title Mother of God (Theotokos) by the Melchite Coptic Egyptians who were well-acquainted with their ancestors' stories of Isis. The Melchite Coptic Egyptians transformed the divine Triad of the Father (Osiris), the Sun (Horus), and the Holy Hathor Cow (Isis) into the Christian trinity of the Father, God (or Jehovah), the Son, Jesus, and the Holy Ghost. It is interesting to note that the Roman Catholic church has such a disdain for women that the Virgin Mary was taken out of the Trinity and in its place this mysterious personality called the "Holy Ghost" was inserted.

Chapter VI told how these changes were consummated at the Council of Chalcedon. At the close of this council meeting, Walter Williams stops using the term A.B.C.E. and uses A.C.E. in order to be historically correct. It is evident that conflicts exist between the chronology of events leading to the formation of Christianity noted by the author and the chronology of events given by theologians and some historians. Such a conflict is inevitable since the author does not lend credence to the union of an icon named Jesus with the title of Christ. The creation of the term A.B.C.E. was necessary to distinguish the Christian theologians chronology of time from actual historical events.

The author recognizes Christ or "Christos" as a title applied to Serapis, a deity invented by the Coptic Melchite Egyptians. Serapis was worshipped by the Greeks and the Romans as the Christ. How could that be if the so-called Jesus Christ was a reality during this time. The term A.B.C.E. was created by the author to denote the time period during and after the supposed life of the character who Christians ascribe to be Jesus up to the time when the author says the title "Christos" or Christ was applied and consummated to and for Serapis (see Glossary). You cannot use the term A.C.E. (or A.D. in Christian terms) until Serapis has been transformed into "The Christ." It is also important to note that at the Council of Chalcedon, there was a new community of Copts being formed. These new Melchites accepted the two natures in Serapis and were called "Dyophysitic Copts." The Dyophysitic Copts were your first community of

Copts who could be called and deemed "Coptic Christians." History applies the name Coptic Christian to all Copts no matter what time era. The term Copt has become synonymous with Christianity. The basic definition of a Copt is simply a hellenized Ancient Egyptian. Hellenization (the Greek culture) was forced on the Ancient Egyptians when Alexander and the Ptolemies invaded Egypt thereby making them Copts. The Copts did not become Christians until after the Melchites made the hypostasis union of the Virgin Theotokos with the Incarnated Logos (Serapis).

Chapter VII deals with the taking back of the Donation of Constantine. The Council of Constantinople II is another significant milestone. Up to now, all the preceding council meetings were called by the Melchites. This council meeting and all other forthcoming council meetings were called by Europeans. At this council meeting, we learned when the world's first Christian and/or Roman Catholic church was built. We also learned who were historically the world's first European and African popes. It is painful to note that when something as destructive as the introduction of a man-made religion has occurred to us as a people, we learn that our own people played a principle role in that destruction. The Uncle Tom-Bourgeois-Dyophysitic-Melchite-Coptic-Egyptian-Christian, Theodore Ascidas, showed Emperor Justinian I how to take back the Donation of Constantine. Justinian was looking for an excuse to take it back. The "Three Nestorian Chapters" were a very weak excuse. The Three Chapters were written years before Justinian was born. Theodore, Theodoret, and Ibas were long dead when Justinian issued his anathemas (544 A.C.E.). Vigilius was set up by Justinian and Theodore Ascidas. Justinian did not build the "Hagia Sophia," the world's first Christian church, for the Exterior Copts or the Melchite Copts. He built it for himself and his wife, Theodora, with the sole purpose of taking back the Donation of Constantine.

In conclusion, permit me to reiterate. Walter Williams needs to be commended for the "New Scholarship" that he has brought forth. I know that what he has revealed goes against most people's spiritual foundation. However, the best medicine does not always taste good going down, but does a world of good once it gets into your system. Be open-minded and hear the message. The message should be clear. It is very important where we invest our natural creator-given spirituality. None of us were born a Christian. Some individual, be it your parents, or someone else close to you, introduced you to this religion called Christianity.

At the time of your birth, the Creator gave you a "Divine Spiritual Birthright" which was hooked up, in place, and in tune with the spiritual rhythm of the universe. We do not need organized religions! The reality of the situation is that all religions are man-made! The Creator provided for our spiritual needs when we were born. Man created religion to try to harness our natural spirituality. Europeans know that people who embrace religions are easy to control and are easily lead. They also became aware many years ago that if they gave the masses a pie-in-the-sky religion under their control, they could then have heaven on earth—with themselves being God.

The scholarly community is now faced with a challenge. Walter Williams has taken investigative research in the field of religious history to a new plateau. This book presents the "New Scholarship" of the Ancient Egyptian Institute. It is definitely a textbook for the study of Christianity. Walter Williams has challenged our old way of thinking with fresh ideas and thoughts. This work is the culmination of nearly twenty years of investigative research. He is definitely the authority on this subject and at the vanguard of raising theological debate to a new dimension. World history in general and religion in particular have been written using the Ancient Egyptians and their descendants as a foundation. This book will be a classic in research scholarship for many years to come.

On a final note, someone once said: "To discover to the world something which deeply concerns it, and of which it was previously ignorant; to prove to it that it had been mistaken on some vital point of temporal or spiritual interest, is as important a service as a human being can render to his fellow creatures, and the most previous gift which could be bestowed on mankind." This is something that the Ancient Egyptians and their descendants have been doing over and over again. Walter Williams has kept this holy legacy going and passes the tradition down to you.

Keep the light of Truth forever shining!

REPERTORY OF SCULPTURE AND FIGURED MONUMENTS RELATING TO THE CULT OF SERAPIS

SERAPIS: BUSTS

Egypt

1. Marble - half figure - no arms - no modius. Cairo Museum.
2. Marble - modius - heavy late work. Cairo Museum.
3. Round plaque of marble - with modius. Cairo Museum.
4. Small. Alexandria Museum.
5. Traces of red color on hair, beard, face. Alexandria Museum No. 23936.
6. With modius - face and beard show traces of gilt. Alexandria Museum No. 22158.

NOTE: Modius--see glossary.

France

7. Parian marble - hair, drapery, chest modern. Louvre.
8. White marble. Near Cairo. Louvre No. 2591.
9. *Small - hard, green stone (basalt) from Egypt - modius with olives. Louvre No. 2590.*
10. *Small - hard, green stone (basalt) - modius broken - from Durand. Louvre No. 2592.*
11. *Hard, green serpentine - modius broken - from Egypt. Louvre No. 2728.*
12. *Head is black, drapery is alabaster - modius lacking but head has a flat piece for modius. Louvre No. 1372.*
13. *Colossal, black marble - modius with olive - retouched. Louvre No. 1370.*
14. *Small, bronze. Cabinet des Medailles.*

Germany

15. *Small. House of Goethe, Weimar.*
16. *Bronze - modius - fillet or band on head. Berlin Museum No. 17583.*
17. *Bronze - modius, ram horns - large hole in head. Berlin Museum No. 11479.*

18. Green basalt patched with bronze. Berlin Museum No. 250.

19. Block of white sandstone, mutilated - found in a bridge at Mainz. Mainz Museum No. 5755.

Great Britain

20. Black marble - some gilt on neck - modius - from Constantinople. British Museum No. 1526.

21. Marble - Zeus - modius is plain. British Museum No. 1527.

22. Marble - Zeus - no modius - eyes are wild-looking. British Museum No. 1528.

23. Black stone with modius, rays - inscription on reverse of plaque - acquired 1929. British Museum.

24. White marble - traces of red color - modius with olives. British Museum No. 1525.

25. Bronze. British Museum No. 944.

26. Marble - with modius - partly restored. Perthshire, Scotland.

Greece

27. Late, poor work - small trace of red color on nose - found in Agora. Agora Excavations Museum, Athens, Inv. 5355.

Italy

28. Fragment - Villa Doria. Pamfilil, Rome.
29. Over life size - from Guastalla. Parma Museum.
30. Small red marble. Rome, Kircher Museum.
31. Helios - cupids on modius - holes in head for metal rays. Florence, Pitti Place.
32. Colossal - pentelic marble - modius and rays modern - found at Colombaro near Frattochie on Via Appia. Vatican Museum, Rotonda No. 549.
33. Fragment of basalt statue - a trace of modius from Palazzo Mattei. Vatican Museum, Sala dei Busti No. 299.

SERAPIS: HEADS

Cyprus

34. Large, - found at Soli in temple along with modius - pieces of Cerberus heads and serpent, probably a sitting statue.

Denmark

35. Mutilated. Museum Thorwaldsen, Copenhagen.

Egypt

36. Antonine, from Arsinoe. Cairo Museum No. 27432.
37. Small. Cairo Museum.
38. Colossal - made of chalk and plaster on top of column. Alexandria Museum No. 3917.
39. Small - photo. Alexandria Museum.
40. Limestone. Alexandria Museum.
41. Time of Antonines. Alexandria Museum.
42. Colossal - found near Pompey's Pillar, Alexandria. Alexandria Museum No. 3914.

43. Front part of colossal head - traces of red color on hair, beard and face - evidences of gilding. Alexandria Museum No. 3912.

France

44. Marble - Jupiter-Serapis - modius wanting - found near Cairo. Louvre No. 2591.
45. Marble - right side of head broken - no modius. Louvre No. 2613.
46. From a terracotta statue - came from Tarsus. Louvre.
47. Pluto. Louvre No. 2259.
48. Colossal - modius has grain and foliage on it traces of red color on beard and hair - from Carthage. Louvre No. 1830.
49. Fragment-of colossal statue - found at Rome in the Tiber. Collection Leopold Goldschmidt.
50. Head of black marble - fragment of a statue - found in Cote-d'Or. Museum of Saint Germain (Dijon).
51. Head of white marble - modius broken - found at Saint-Didier (Vaucluse). Avignon, Musee Calvet.

Germany

52. No modius - marble. Berlin Museum No. 251.
53. Marble - from Rome. Berlin Museum No. 252.
54. Alabaster - is this a bust? Berlin Museum No. 253.
55. Alabaster. Berlin Museum No. 254.
56. No modius - marble. Berlin Museum No. 255.
57. Terracotta. Vienna Museum.
58. Small - bought in Egypt for Prince Ruprecht of Bavaria.

Great Britain

59. Marble - from temple of Puteoli - face is weathered - modius gone. British Museum No. 1529.
60. Marble - plain modius - right side broken. British Museum No. 1530.
61. Mutilated - flat piece on head with dowel hole. British Museum No. 1957.

62. With rays - from Via Appia, Rome. Ince, Blundell Hall.
63. Small, alabaster. Ince, Blundell Hall.

Greece

64. From a statue - red color on hair, beard and face - gilt on beard - found at Corinth by excavation. Corinth Museum.
65. From acrolithic statue - gilt on face, hair and beard. Corinth Museum.
66. Colossal - red color on hair and beard - found in Serapeum at Thessalonica. Thessalonica Museum No. 897.
67. Marble - found at Delos by excavation. Delos Museum.

Italy

68. Large, ornate. Rome Museum.
69. Double life size. Rome Museum (Museum number desired)
70. Small - on a statue of Zeus. Rome, Villa Albani.

71. Fragment of colossal green basalt on a black marble bust. Volla Albani, Galleria diCanopo.
72. Over life size. No modius. Palazzo Colonna.
73. Small. Palazzo Colonna.
74. Torlonia Museum.
75. Torlonia Museum.
76. Characteristic moustache - modius with tree and grain. Garden of Palazzo Barberini.
77. Black basalt. Palazzo Guistiniani.
78. Large head - labelled "Giove, arte romana" - from Milan - traces of red color on hair, beard and face - traces of gilt on face - no modius. Milan.
79. Marble - no modius. Florence, Cortile of Palazzo Riccardi-Medici.
80. Pisa - Campo Santo - North Corridor - outer wall.
81. Small - modius broken. Venice., Torcello.
82. Parma, Museo di Autichita.

Turkey

83. Istanbul Museum No. 1226.

SERAPIS: SEATED STATUES

Egypt

84. Made of wood - body is red and black - on hair, face, beard and neck is white plaster coat gilded. Alexandria Museum no. 23352.
85. Small - found at Alexandria. Alexandria Museum.
86. Marble - head, left arm and part of right gone. Alexandria Museum No. 3913.
87. Marble - left arm and part of right gone - modius and Cerberus wanting. Alexandria Museum No. 3916.

France

88. Modius, Cerberus right, staff left - snake on throne - applique in bronze. Louvre No. 326.

Germany

89. Terracotta - left raised, right on Cerberus - modius on throne. Berlin Museum No. 9167.

Great Britain

90. Bronze - from Paramythia. British Museum No. 276 (Bronze Room)
91. Statuette - restored. Lansdowne House.
92. Luna marble - modius, Cerberus, staff - much restored. Ince, Blundell Hall.
93. Almost same as No. 87. Ince Blundell Hall.
94. Silver statuette - Cornucopia in left. Collection Payne-Knight.

Italy

95. Luna marble. Pio-Clementino.
96. Greek marble - scepter in left, right on Cerberus - found at puteoli in ruins of a monument called Temple of Serapis. Naples.

97. Right on scepter, left on Cerberus. Museum Capitolini, Rome.
98. Headless statue of Serapis type dedicated to Serapis. Turin.

NOTE: <u>Cerberus</u>--see glossary.

SERAPIS: STANDING STATUES

Egypt

99. May be Serapis veiled figure of stone. Cairo Museum No. 1016.

France

100. Bronze statuette. Cabinet des Medailles.
101. Standing figure of Italian marble - fragment of a table - right arm is gone, cornucopia in left modius - Cerberus is at right - found at Chiragan by excavation. Toulouse Museum No. 891.

Great Britain

102. Bronze - from Rhodes. British Museum.
103. Much restored. Castle Howard, Yorkshire.

Italy

104. Relief on marble plaque - modius - right raised, left at side - figure is standing in a doorway. Turin.
105. Bronze statuette. Florence.
106. Mutilated - in gray marble - over life-size - restored as Athena. Villa Albani, garden behind Casino.

GLOSSARY OF TERMS

A.B.C.E. The term "A.B.C.E." (or "After B.C.E.") is used by the author to denote the time when B.C.E. ended, and includes the time until the close of the Council of Chalcedon (451 A.B.C.E.). At this point, the Christian Era officially began; therefore, "A.C.E." or (After the Christian Era) can then be correctly used. Thus, in order to be historically correct, the term "After B.C.E." was invented by the author.

A.C.E. After the Christian Era.

Alexander, The Greek Alexander, called "The Great" by some, but called "The Greek" by the author. He cannot be great because he cut off the culture of the Ancient Egyptians.

Apotheosize   To make into a god.

Arianist   A follower of Arius who taught that Serapis was a created creature.

B.C.E.   Before the Christian Era.

Cerberus   In Greek and Roman mythology, the three-headed dog guarding the gate of Hades.

Coptic   A Coptic Egyptian who accepted
Christian   the Dyophysitic Union at the Council of Ephesus.

Coptic   A direct descendant of the Ancient
Egyptian   Egyptians.

Dyophysitic   Divine spirit and human nature combining both into one. The Coptic Egyptians accepting this union were called Christians.

Exterior Coptic
Egyptians   A name invented by the author to designate Coptic Egyptians who did not accept Serapis as God. They

are referred to by the author as the "Exterior Coptic Religious Community" beginning in 320 B.C.E. They were "exterior" because they refused to accept the image of Serapis as God which caused Ptolemy I, Lagi to close all of their temples. With their temples closed, this caused them to become exterior. Later, during the Byzantine Era, they were referred to as "Arianists" or "Monophysites," and in today's history books, they are incorrectly referred to as Christians and Jews. They are also referred to by the author as the Coptic Primitive Holiness, puritan martyred exterior religions community during this time in history.

Euthyches A Monophysite Coptic Egyptian (see Monophysite) who recognized the one nature in Serapis/Christ during and after the Council of Ephesus. Also known as the founder of Monophysitism.

Homoousios
Creed   A creed developed at the Council of Niceae I (325 A.B.C.E.), known also as the "Nicene Creed," designating, of or holding the theory that God the Father (Osiris) and God the Son (Serapis) are identical in substance.

Jacobite   A name derived from the Nestorian semi-Monophysite Coptic Egyptian Christian "Jacob Baradaeus" (a.k.a. James Baradai). The man who taught the heathen European Arabs Monophysite Christianity that later evolved into the pagan religion called Islam.

Logos   In Christian theology meaning "The Word."

Melchite   A Coptic Egyptian who created and accepted the European icon/image of Serapis as a God, as opposed to the Coptic Egyptians who did not accept Serapis as God.

Melchite Papa   A member of the Melchite Coptic Religious Community beginning with Sylvester I who received from Constantine the Donation of Constantine which made the receiver of this donation the head Papa of the Melchites. Also, any member of the Melchite Coptic Religious Community who was elected to succeed in that capacity after Sylvester I.

Modius   Serapis was often depicted wearing on his head a grain modius which is a round tubular cup containing seeds of grain. This gave the creature Serapis the assimilated characteristics of Osiris, ancient Egyptian god of vegetation.

Monophysite   A person who believes that Serapis/Christ had only one nature, a divine Osiris-like spirit only, but did not believe Serapis/Christ had a human nature.

Nestorian   A follower of Nestorius, a Syrian Coptic quasi-Monophysite/Christian (see Monophysite) who did not accept the creature the Virgin Mary as the "Theotokos" (see Theotokos).

Papa   A father or patriarch, a person with the position of authority over the Melchite religious community.

See   The official seat or center of authority of a bishop or patriarch, the first See was the Hagia Sophia.

Serapis   A man-created composite god, a link between the Ancient Egyptian god "Osiris" and the sacred bull of Memphis, "Apis," created by the priest society at Memphis, Egypt (320 B.C.E.).

She/He Creator A term used by the author which recognizes the Creator as having two genes (female and male) which gives the Creator cosmic balance.

Ptolemy   A Greek ruler of Egypt.

Theotokos   A title given to the created-creature the Virgin Mary meaning the Mother of God (Serapis/Christ) at the Council of Ephesus (431 A.B.C.E.).

Vicar   A Ptolemy or Roman Emperor regarded as the representative of "Serapis/Christ." Today, the Roman Catholic Pope is regarded as the earthly representative of Christ.

APPENDIX

WHY THE MEDU-NETCHER-HIEROGLYPHICS HAVE NEVER BEEN DECIPHERED

Contrary to the teachings of Western institutions, the medu-netcher or hieroglyphics, which are the pictorial symbols of the Ancient Egyptians, have never been deciphered. The following are the reasons.

- In order for the medu-netcher or hieroglyphs to have been deciphered, one would have had to ask the Ancient Egyptians who drew the symbols what he/she meant for them to be.

- To illustrate my point, I will draw a symbol of my own creation:

  I now ask, what is the meaning of this symbol? Realistically, you cannot know until I provide you with the meaning.

- No one can put a phonetic alphabetical value to symbols. For example, the symbol of the question mark (?); can you assign a phonetic alphabetical value such as the letters T, M, P, K, R, etc., to the question mark? The answer is "no" because the question mark is telling you something to do, to question!

- If you drive a car, you were tested in three categories: eyesight, rules of the road, and symbols. When you were tested for symbols, you were asked what the symbols were telling you to do. In order to know what the symbols are telling one to do one has to know the meaning of the symbols as standardized by the Division of Motor Vehicles. If you did not know the meaning of the symbols, you failed the test.

- Also one cannot use any language (Coptic or otherwise) as a key to understanding the symbols of the hieroglyphs, i.e., you cannot apply a language or languages to symbols that one does not know the meaning of.

• It is impossible to reduce 400 or more symbols of the hieroglyphs to 26 letters of an alphabetical system.

• What the Europeans did was to decide which hieroglyphic symbols would be used to represent a given letter of the alphabet (i.e., they matched and assigned letters of the alphabet to the hieroglyphic symbols of their choice).

The arbitrary assigning of letters to symbols is evident with the acceptance of the pioneering works of J.J. Barthelemy, Count Silvestre de Sacy, Johan Akerblad, Thomas Young, and later, of Jean François Champollion by the majority of Western academia. In 1822, Champollion, with the help of the works of Thomas Young and the Rosetta Stone, established a supposed system, theories, and principles for deciphering the Ancient Egyptian hieroglyphs. His work at first was not accepted by other European scholars until another stone with bilingual inscriptions, the decree of Canopus, was discovered in 1866. This stone was believed to have confirmed the theories of Champollion.

Questions:

(1)   After 44 years of widespread disagree-
       ment among the European scholars, how
       did the discovery of the Stone of Canopus
       in 1866 confirm Champollion's theories
       and readings of the hieroglyphs?

(2)   Where is the original Stone of Canopus?

(3)   Who discovered the Canopus Stone?

(4)   How was the Canopus Stone discovered?

(5)   Who validated the authenticity of the
       Stone of Canopus?

Champollion's accepted work on the
hieroglyphs inspired Adolph Erman, then curator of
Ancient Egyptian artifacts at the Berlin Museum.
Erman was a student of Carl Richard Lepsius,
German Egyptologist, who encouraged him to publish
a grammatical dictionary of the hieroglyphs in 1880.
The dictionary was revised in 1925 and finished in
1934. Erman's work created a new pseudo-direction
and language for the Ancient Egyptian hieroglyphs.
His work inspired and gave E.A. Wallis Budge a

guide line to write his book entitled "The Book of the Dead" or "The Coming Forth by Day and by Night." I urge you to read this appendix over and over again until you understand the reasons why the medu-netcher or hieroglyphs have never been deciphered. I will now conclude by quoting from the book "The Rosetta Stone" written for the British Museum by Carol Andrews:

> "It is not possible, strictly speaking, to compile an alphabet of hieroglyphic signs. For practical purposes, however, certain unilateral hieroglyphics have been selected to form a kind of alphabet which is universally used for the organization of dictionaries, word lists, index and for general reference purposes." As one can see, it is not possible to use the Rosetta Stone as an instrument to decipher the Ancient Egyptian hieroglyphs. Warning: Do not allow European scholars or Western institution-trained African scholars to tell you that the Ancient Egyptian hieroglyphs have been deciphered.

Walter Williams

BIBLIOGRAPHY

1. Andrews, Carol, *Rosetta Stone*. Peter Bedrick, New York, New York.

2. Bowman, Alan K., *Egypt After the Pharaohs*. University of California Press, 1986.

3. Brady, T.A., *Serapis and Isis.* Collected Essays. Ares Publishers, Inc., Chicago, Illinois.

4. Budge, E.A. Wallis, *The Rosetta Stone*. Ares Publishers, Inc., Chicago, Illinois.

5. Doane, T.W., *Bible Myths and Their Parallels in Other Religions*. Truth Seeker Company, Inc., San Diego, California.

6. Goudy, Frederick, W., *The Alphabet and Element of Lettering*. Dover Publication, New York, 1918-1942.

7. Hall, Manly P., *Free Masonry of the Ancient Egyptians*. The Philosophical Research Society Inc., Los Angeles, California.

8. King, Charles, *Hieroglyphics to Alphabet.* Crane Russak Co., Inc., New York, 1927.

9. Kinross, Lord, and the editors of the Newsweek Book Division, **Hagia Sophia.** *Newsweek.* New York, 1972.

10. Lodge, M.D., G. Henry, *The History of Ancient Art, Vol. II.* Translated from the German version by John Winkelmann, James R. Osgood and Company, Boston, Massachusetts., 1873.

11. Lurker, Manfred, *The Gods and Symbols of Ancient Egypt.* Thames and Hudson, Inc., 500 Fifth Avenue, New York, New York.

12. McKenzie, John L., S.J., *Dictionary of the Bible.* New York: MacMillan Publishing Co., Inc. and London: Collier MacMillan Publishers, 1965.

13. Mercatante, Anthony S., *Who's Who in Egyptian Mythology.* Clarkson N. Potter, Inc. Publishers, New York. Distributed by Crown Publishers, Inc.

14. Murnane, William J., *The Penguin Guide to Ancient Egypt.* Viking Penguin, Inc., 40 West 23 Street, New York, New York 10010, U.S.A.

15. Nazir-Ali, Michael, *Islam: A Christian Perspective.*   The   Westminster   Press, Philadelphia, Pennsylvania, 1983.

16. Solmsen, Friedrich. *Isis Among the Greeks and the Romans.* Published for Oberlin College by Harvard University Press, Cambridge, Massachusetts and London, England.

17. Stewart, Desmond and the editors of Time-Life Books, *Early Islam.* Time-Life Books, New York.

18. Van Loon, Hendrik, *The Story of Mankind.* Star Books, Garden City Publishing, Inc., Garden City, New York.

19. Wells, H.G., *The Outline of History.* Garden City, New York: Garden City Books, Volume I, 1920.

20. Whiter, Walter, *Universal Etymological Dictionary: On a New Plan.* Cambridge University Press, 1822.

21. Woodson, Carter G. *The Mis-Education of the Negro.* Africa World Press, Inc., P.O. Box 1892, Trenton, New Jersey 08618.

22. *Gods of Egypt in the Graeco-Roman Period, The.* Kelsey Museum of Archaeology, the University of Michigan, Ann Arbor.

23. *New Catholic Encyclopedia,* 1967. The Catholic University Press of America, Washington, D.C.

24. *New Encyclopedia Britannica, The,* 1987 edition.

25. Standard American Encyclopedia, The, 1937 edition. Standard American Corporation, Chicago, Illinois.

INDEX

PAGE

PAGE

PAGE

PAGE

NOTE: Contact the author for lectures, radio and television interviews.

E-Mail: ancientegyptian@msn.com

NOTES

NOTES

NOTES

NOTES